GREAT CYCL[ES]
YORKS[HIRE]

DORIAN SPEAKMAN

DIAL
HOUSE

First published 2000

ISBN 0 7110 2706 4

© Dorian Speakman 2000

Published by Dial House

an imprint of Ian Allan Publishing Ltd,
Terminal House, Shepperton, Surrey TW17 8AS.
Printed by Ian Allan Printing Ltd, Riverdene
Business Park, Hersham, Surrey KT12 4RG.

Code: 0004/E

Front cover: Fountains Abbey. *Author*

Front cover, inset: Londesborough village, East
Yorkshire Wolds. *Colin Speakman*

Title page: Flamborough Head cliffs. *Author*

This page: Ingleborough from near Eldroth.
Colin Speakman

CONTENTS 3

GREAT CYCLE ROUTES IN YORKSHIRE

The county of Yorkshire, with all its diversity, offers great opportunities for the cyclist. From the high moors and dales of the Pennines and North York Moors, to the flat plain of the Vale of York, the rolling chalk hills of the Wolds and the dramatic east coast, there are available great varieties of terrain and attractions. Many of the places mentioned in this book may already be familiar, but others, which may seem inaccessible, are within comparatively easy reach with the aid of the region's railway network.

This book is aimed at the cyclist with some experience who would like to know more about what is possible for a day trip. The routes chosen are along mostly quiet back roads or tracks in beautiful countryside and include some of the most interesting attractions that Yorkshire has to offer. It assumes that the reader has some experience of cycling although the routes devised are meant for a mix of abilities and experience, ranging from a pleasant short afternoon's ride to a full day's excursion. Some of the routes interlink, and so it is also possible to use this book as a guide to help plan part of a longer cycling tour using the quiet back routes to explore Yorkshire. Some of the routes can also be shortened and on these a cut-off point has been included from which public transport is available.

For that reason, few of the rides are concentrated in urban areas — the train is used to get the cyclist away from the maze of urban streets and highways and straight out into the countryside. The rides are mostly linear in nature — getting the most from the ride out; the train is there for the return trip home!

The routes and connecting rail services have all been tested, but please bear in mind that over time councils can change road junctions, new cycle tracks can appear and so on. The following cycle routes are simply a selection of what is on offer — hopefully they will inspire readers to explore the corners of Yorkshire on their own, armed with a map and a rail timetable!

Acknowledgements
My thanks to Colin Speakman for his help in gathering material on the various places in the region and for his suggestions for some of the routes.

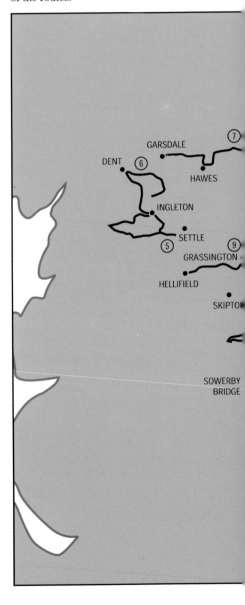

ON/OFF-ROAD

Some routes (and all of Route 16) have some off-road sections and are therefore traffic free, which is ideal if you are getting used to cycling again after a long gap. The Trans-Pennine Trail in the Don Valley has a surface of smooth gravel but (at the time of writing) the Leeds branch along the Aire & Calder Canal (Route 24) is mainly footpath. Note that the South Holderness route (11) and a few with short bridlepath sections (such as Routes 3, 19, 20, 22, 23 and 24) may become muddy after wet weather. For these routes, bikes with thicker-tread tyres are more suitable (and so are mudguards!).

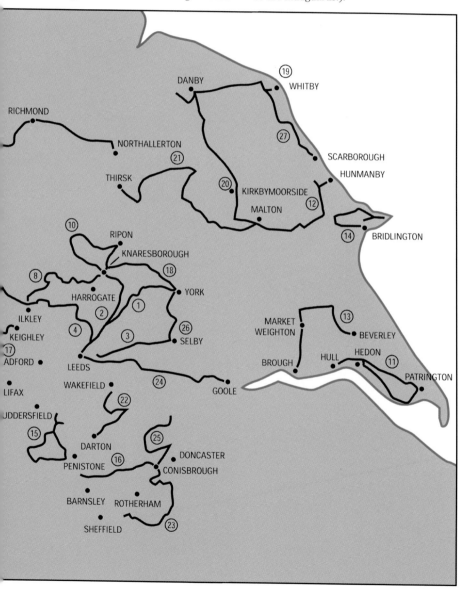

Above: Confering on
which way to go.
Sustrans/Julia Bayne

Left: Sustrans path,
north of York. *Author*

Right: Gentle
gradients make for
easy going. *Sustrans/
Martin Herron*

THE NATIONAL CYCLE NETWORK

Sustrans, the national cycling charity, has been creating a National Cycle Network throughout Britain. The National Cycle Network aims to achieve a high quality network of safe and attractive routes on a combination of totally traffic-free paths, protected sections of cycle track on minor roads, and quiet back roads and byways. The project will be completed by 2005, but already a good part of the network is in place.

On several of the routes you will come across and use some parts of the National Cycle Network — sections of the Hull and York to Middlesbrough routes, and the Trans-Pennine Trail running from Hornsea and Hull to Doncaster, Barnsley and the Upper Don Valley over the Pennines to Manchester, Liverpool and Southport. You will get to recognise the blue signs for the National Cycle Route, but note that for some rides, such as those in the Howardian Hills or the southern Wolds, the National Cycle Route is only met briefly.

PRACTICAL POINTS
Planning Your Trip

If you are relatively new to cycling, or have not cycled much apart from very short trips, make a note of the terrain and distance. It is best to start on some of the easier, flatter routes and build yourself up gradually.

The selection of rides is designed to make maximum use of back roads where traffic is light, but does assume that you (and any children accompanying you) have some experience of road traffic. In certain sections some roads are busier, and these are mentioned in the text.

What to Take
— Check List
• Cycle repair kit (including a spare inner tube);
• Pump;
• Waterproofs;
• Water bottle;
• Suntan cream (essential on a sunny day; it is amazing how quickly legs, arms and necks can burn);
• Insect repellent (useful if cycling through a forest in summer, when midges and mosquitoes can be rampant!);
• Food; either snack or packed lunch;
• Lock;
• Money;
• Hand wipes (great for getting oil off your hands after an unexpected repair);
• Lights/reflective belt (essential if there is the remotest chance you will be out after dusk);
• Map/guide book (OS Landranger maps are used for the routes in this book);
• Hat/gloves.

Always take an emergency set of tools, so that you can repair a puncture or make adjustments to your bike while on the road. This should include a pump, inner tube, Allen keys, adjustable spanner, screwdriver, tyre levers (at least two) and chain link remover, and a puncture repair kit.

Carrying the Essentials

The expected weather for the day and the length of time you expect to be out will influence how much you will want to carry with you on your bike. The easiest way of carrying things is with panniers which attach to a metal carrier on the rear of the bike. Whenever possible, avoid carrying things on

Left: Sustrans cycleway sign and wind vane, near Skelton, York. *Author*

Below: Hornsea Rail Trail, near Keyingham, Holderness. *Author*

your back — a rucksack can not only be a strain on the back but can throw the cyclist off balance, perhaps with disastrous effect. Alternatively, for short trips in good weather, a saddle bag which can be attached to the rear of a saddle may be enough for tools and small items of food.

Before you leave home, check the following on your bike:

- **Brakes:** check front and back brakes are working. Also check that the cables and brake blocks are not worn, otherwise they will require replacement.
- **Tyres:** check tyres are properly pumped up hard and that the tread is not worn or the valves damaged, otherwise the tyre or inner tube may need replacing. There is now a fluid available that is pumped into inner tubes (so far only available for mountain bike inner tubes) that can counter punctures. Otherwise it is possible to get inner tubes made from tougher material.
- **Chain:** check it is well oiled and not slack.
- **Saddle:** check it is the right height, so that you can touch the ground with your toes when sitting in the saddle, but that it is high enough to have your legs almost straight when pedalling. This is particularly important for children's bikes.
- **Gears:** check these are working. If in need of more than minor adjustments, they will usually require the attention of a bike shop.
- **Wheels:** check for broken spokes or buckled wheels. If damaged, the bike will need to go to a shop for repair.
- **Lights:** check they are working (back and front) and not in need of a new battery or bulb.
- **Bell:** have one fitted — and use it to warn walkers and other cyclists on a cycle path when you approach.

Make sure you know how to fix a puncture: the ubiquitous broken glass of British urban areas is a curse for today's cyclist. Most puncture repair kits have clear instructions on the back of the box to help you — but you might practice removing and replacing a tyre and inner tube before you have to do it in the pouring rain on a remote hillside.

In hot weather it is advisable to take at least one litre of water, and to buy drinks en route. Whilst you can always buy food on the trip, also have some sandwiches and energy food like flapjacks to keep you going.

Lock Up!
Bicycle thefts are on the increase, even in rural areas, so even if you are intending to stop for only a short time, it is advisable to lock your bike up, if only to avoid yourself being stranded in a remote location! Always try to lock your bike to something, preferably a solid object such as a lamp post or fence. The best type of locks to use are the reinforced black steel U-locks which require special equipment to cut them open without a key. Other types of lock are easily removed by enterprising thieves using bolt cutters. It is also advisable to have a record of your frame identity number, so that in the event of your bike being stolen, you have some chance of recovering it.

Left: Clapham. *Author*

Below Right: Smiling makes the going easy. *Sustrans/Julia Bayne*

Having said that, keep the weight down, as you may well have to climb steps with the bike at a station. If you are riding in dusky or dark conditions it is a good idea to be wearing light or reflective clothing to make yourself more visible.

A well-fitted bike helmet is advisable for any cycling trip, as the head is the most crucial area of the body to protect. A helmet has the advantage of keeping off some of the rain in wet weather, or reducing the effects of a cold headwind!

Access to Stations

This book does assume that there is relatively easy cycling access to your local railway station. York, Hull and Leeds councils have produced cycling maps to make the job easier — you can get the maps at local book stores or from the city councils' cycling departments. If you find that access is not good enough to your station then please write a letter to the council's Highways Department, and contact your local cycling group — change is possible but only if you act!

Another point to bear in mind is that on many stations platform access is via steps — so look out for lifts or be prepared to carry your bike.

Clothing and Footwear

Spare clothing in layers is useful in case the weather turns for the worse, or during the return journey the evening is cool. You do not have to go to the expense of buying designer cycle wear — it is preferable to wear natural fibres that allow the skin to breathe. A foldable lightweight waterproof is useful too.

Stretchable trousers or leggings which are tight at the leg are ideal for cycling; avoid baggy tracksuits which can easily be caught in the chain and thick non-stretch material like denim on a longer ride which can get very uncomfortable when the seams rub the inside of your leg. The best all-route solution for those intending to do a lot of cycling is a pair of padded cycling shorts, which do provide excellent protection against saddle-sore behinds. For footwear any reasonably hard-wearing flat-soled shoe is suitable.

Using your Car

Despite the aim of this book to encourage the use of the cycle as much as possible, you may find that the only way to get your bike(s) to the nearest station is to use a car to transport them.

A popular method is to use a back carrier which is fitted to the car using a combination of straps, clips and adjustable angles. This type of rack usually carries two bikes. Another method of carrying bikes on the outside of the car is to use a roofrack designed to carry bikes. Some are designed to carry the bikes upside down and others the right way up. The advantage of this system is that it does not restrict the driver's rear view, but it can affect the car's wind resistance and you need to be pretty strong to lift your bike on to the roof, especially if it's a heavy mountain bike.

Another option, used by some motorists, is to carry the bikes in the back of an estate car or larger hatchback. Quick release wheels means that most bikes will fit into the back of a car, though it may restrict the number of passengers you can carry with you.

BIKES ON TRAINS
Bike Rail
Taking your bike by rail opens up a whole new range of possibilities for cycle rides. Trains provide a good way of avoiding city traffic when getting out to the countryside, and the vast majority of trains in Yorkshire carry cycles for free (see below).

Planning Your Day
It is as well to make sure you have plenty of time for your ride, so if you are booking a

return train (see below) make sure you have given yourself at least an hour extra to take account of any mishaps, or tiredness at the end of a long ride. Make sure you have a timetable handy (leaflets available at stations) in case you miss your intended train.

Reservations and Costs
Just about all local trains running on the routes described in this book are run by Northern Spirit — which does not charge for the carriage of cycles on trains. However, space is limited; often only two bikes can be carried per train. Northern Spirit also requests that bookings should be made on Trans-Pennine Express services which run on the Huddersfield-Leeds-Scarborough/Hull/Middlesbrough routes. It is also a good idea to reserve a place on the Leeds-Settle-Carlisle or Leeds-Lancaster services as train services are limited, particularly off season. You can make reservations at any staffed station. The other carriers, Virgin and GNER, do charge for cycle carriage, so this is only worth it if you are travelling long distances from outside Yorkshire — in Yorkshire there are many local slower trains that can be used as an alternative.

Above: Castleton station, Eskdale.
Colin Speakman

Right: Shady walled lane at Woodsetts, near the Nottinghamshire border. *Author*

Bike Storage

On Trans-Pennine services the units usually have bike storage between the carriages — look out for a bike symbol on the doors. On local trains space is provided for cycles or wheelchairs at one end of the train, otherwise the seats can be tipped up at each end of the train; you might have to ask for the seat to be vacated! If space is tight it may help to invert the front wheel. On the Ilkley and Skipton/Keighley trains, older electric units still run at the time of writing and bikes can be stored in the guard's compartment in the centre of the train.

Many stations now provide cycle parking either in lockers or on Sheffield stands which is useful if you wish to leave your bike before you catch your train.

Getting the Best Fare for Your Trip

In West Yorkshire the Rail Day Rover is useful for riders starting their journey from West Yorkshire. This would include rides such as Sowerby Bridge-Keighley, Leeds-Ilkley, Stocksmoor-Don Valley-Shepley, Darton-Sandal & Agbrigg.

In South Yorkshire the Travelmaster ticket covers all train journeys within the county and is useful for rides such as Silkstone Common-Conisbrough or Kiveton Park-Doncaster.

On the longer distance routes and those which are a long way from home you might wish to consider getting a North Country Rail Rover, which avoids the need to buy costly single tickets for rides such as Garsdale-Northallerton or Malton-Danby. This allows you to travel four days out of eight, all over the network from Leeds to Hull, and Hebden Bridge to Lancaster, Carlisle and Newcastle. (The cost is £55 until 27 May 2000 and is "unlikely to change much in price.") With a bit of planning you can make some interesting cycle rides not normally possible; in addition you could link the routes or use the Rover ticket to explore a completely different part of the county. On other routes, a Supersaver Return (not valid Fridays) or Day Return with an appropriate add-on single may be the best option. The staff at your nearest booking office should be able to help.

LOCAL CYCLING GROUPS

There are many cycling groups in the region and these can be contacted either by the National Cyclists Touring Club (see 'Useful Addresses') or through other groups which appear in local authority cycle guides (see 'Further Information').

LEEDS TO YORK VIA THORNER, BRAMHAM, THORP ARCH AND HEALAUGH

After climbing out of Leeds and the Aire Valley, then dipping into the lower reaches of the Wharfe Valley, this route runs through the low rolling country on the edge of the Vale of York. The final run into York is along the traffic-free riverside cycle track.

The first route description is the link from Leeds station to Roundhay Park, taking the best route in terms of clarity and traffic conditions (Ordnance Survey's *Leeds Cycling Map* is useful). The route runs northeast through Sheepscar, through the edge of Harehills and Chapeltown (using back streets to avoid major junctions on Roundhay Road), via Oakwood to the park.

BACKGROUND AND PLACES OF INTEREST:

Roundhay Park and Thorner
(see Route 2)

Bramham
An extremely attractive village in the heart of the Magnesian Limestone country, now mercifully bypassed by the A1. Georgian architecture and mellow stonework, together with typical rolling countryside of scattered woodland and low hills, make this an extremely attractive area. Bramham Park has a fine Queen Anne house and one of the finest examples in England of an elaborate landscaped garden in the French manner of King Louis XIV.

Clifford Church
One of the most impressive Victorian churches in Yorkshire, it was built in grand Romanesque style in 1845-8 with a tower added in 1859/60. Money for this unusual Roman Catholic church was subscribed by the Pope, the Queen of Sardinia and the Grand Duke of Palma.

Boston Spa
The discovery of magnesian and sulphur springs, believed to be a cure for gout and rheumatism, along the Wharfe riverside in the early 18th century, led to the development of this little spa town on the once important turnpike road between Wetherby and York. By the 19th century it was overtaken in popularity by Harrogate, but many old spa buildings and inns remain.

York
One of Europe's great medieval walled cities, York is a treasurehouse of Roman, Viking, medieval and Georgian architecture, with several nationally important museums, including the National Railway Museum, the Yorkshire Museum and Jorvik, as well as one of England's greatest cathedrals. There is also a wonderful network of central streets, squares and alleyways to explore, containing shops, boutiques, cafés and pubs. It is also Britain's most cycle-friendly city with a network of traffic-free routes in and out of the city centre and along the banks of the Ouse, for both utilitarian and leisure cycling.

Starting Point: (Leeds) Roundhay Park.

Finish/Return Point: York; frequent rail services from York to Leeds and other centres (MetroTrain York and Selby line).

Distance: 41km (25 miles) from Roundhay Park, 47km (29 miles) from Leeds railway station.

Maps: Ordnance Survey (OS) Landranger 104 Leeds & Bradford; OS 105 York & Selby; Leeds Cycling Map.

Surfaces and Gradients: Rolling gentle hill country as far as Bramham, then progressively flatter countryside. Minor roads and lanes and a tarmac cycle path.

Traffic Conditions: From Leeds station to Roundhay Park: Beware of buses in the city centre section; traffic can be busy along

This route links
Leeds city centre
with Roundhay Park.
Although not ideal in
terms of traffic
levels, it gives a
reasonably safe
route to the park for
those not within
easy reach of
northeast Leeds.
From Leeds

North Street and Roundhay Road, but back
roads are used where possible. Care will be
needed when navigating.
From Roundhay Park: Generally quiet roads
or lanes but some care required in York city
centre when accessing the station.

Facilities: Cafés: Roundhay Park, Boston
Spa, several in York.
Pubs: Thorner (3), Bramham, Boston Spa,
Wighill, York (several).
WCs: Roundhay Park (above café by
Waterloo Lake), York station, Yorkshire
Museum.

Top: Bramham village. *Author*

Below: Granary Wharf canal basin, below Leeds
station. *Colin Speakman*

railway station head for the main entrance.
Turn left and keep to the right side, going as
far as the junction. Using the pedestrian
crossing, cross the road on the right, then
cross Boar Lane (on the left) and turn right.

Take the next left, Lower Basinghall
Street, past the pedestrian zone that splits
the street, to the Headrow at the top. Where
traffic is directed to turn left, instead turn
right, using the cobbled traffic island
(caution!), and at the traffic lights go
straight ahead down the slope. At the next
junction turn left up Briggate, past the
theatre. At the traffic lights, keep straight
ahead, ignoring turn-offs left and right.
Continue down North Street as far as the
Sheepscar Interchange.

Using the toucan crossing, head for the
island ahead to the
right and join the
cycle/bus lane to pass
the taxi rank to the
lights at the opposite
end. Cross the road
and pass the Thomas
Danby College before
joining Roundhay
Road (use the pelican
crossing just further
to the right if traffic
is too busy).

Turn right on to
Roundhay Road
(caution, traffic
turning in different

ROUTE
LEEDS STATION - ROUNDHAY PARK

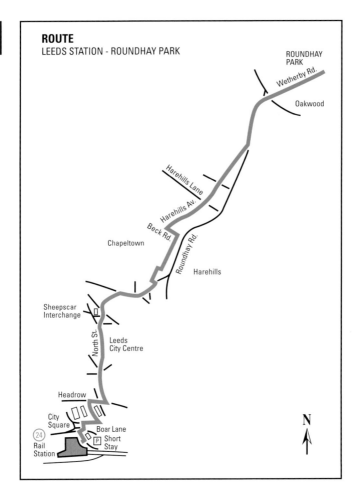

Roundhay Park -York
From Roundhay Park South Exit (Wetherby Road) take Wetherby Road towards the A58 and Wetherby. Turn left at the junction and follow the A58 for a short distance up the hill before taking the next right (caution!). Take the next left, up the hill, to the roundabout on the hilltop.

Turn left to Monkswood Gate and the ring road (caution!). Use the split road crossing to cross to the street opposite. Go along Ringwood Drive to the end. Turn right and go along the straight, crossing over Coal Road until the road ends at a T-junction. Turn left to Thorner.

From Thorner Main Street continue through the village; after the double bend by the church the road climbs quite steeply before gently descending by the grounds of Bramham Park and ascending the other side of the valley. Continue to Bramham crossing the A1 and turn right then left after the bridge to descend into the village. Go right at the old stone cross at Bramham and take the lane up Town Hill. Turn left at the top, then take the second left on the sharp bend on to Windmill Lane. Follow this lane down the hill into Clifford. Turn left then right by Clifford church taking the road to its end in Boston Spa.

directions at the next junction) and continue almost until the traffic lights on the hill — turn right just before. Go down Gathorne Terrace, then turn right on a concrete path to Bank Side Street. At the crossroads continue along Hill Top Mount as far as Beck Road, almost at the end of the street, and turn left. Follow Beck Road until it meets Harehills Avenue at the end.

Follow Harehills Avenue through the traffic lights until it joins Roundhay Road, then continue on Roundhay Road up to Oakwood. At the traffic lights go straight ahead; the south entrance of Roundhay Park appears on the left after $\frac{1}{2}$km ($\frac{1}{4}$ mile).

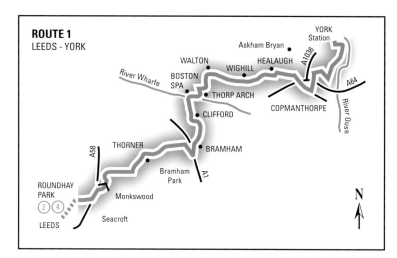

ROUTE 1
LEEDS - YORK

Turn right on to the Main Street before turning left (signed for British Library) over the narrow bridge across the River Wharfe and into Thorp Arch. Take the next right, soon passing the prison. Turn right at the next junction and keep to this lane as it passes through the small villages of Wighill and Healaugh. Continue for the next 5km (3 miles) until the junction near Askham Bryan — turn right to go to the roundabout above the A64. Take the bridge over the dual carriageway and follow the lane into Copmanthorpe; take the first turn left into this suburban village. Where the road meets the A64, there is a special crossing for cyclists and pedestrians to go straight ahead to a cycle path which soon veers off the main road. Heading towards York, the path meets traffic lights — at the second set use these to cross over and turn back (ignore the signed route into York city centre) to take the route signed for Selby.

Follow this path round as it dips down the slope; below the bridge the quieter route into York is signed 'City Centre 3'. This next stage is well signed — the path crosses a field and then York Racecourse before dropping down to the river bank of the Ouse and into the city centre.

The route takes minor streets running parallel with the river. At the traffic lights continue straight ahead until you reach North Street. To reach the railway station from the

end of North Street turn on to the inner ring road and follow round for 100m, keeping to the left. The station is on the right.

Below: Clifford church, near Boston Spa. *Author*

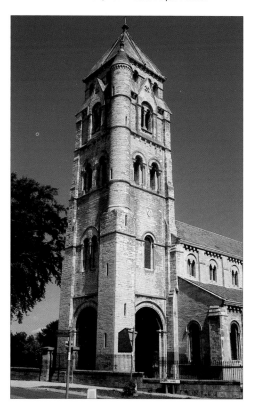

LEEDS TO KNARESBOROUGH VIA THORNER, WETHERBY AND SPOFFORTH

The route runs over rolling countryside through the surprisingly lovely outskirts of northeast Leeds, past open fields and small secluded woodlands, and ends in the spectacular lower Nidd gorge which is overlooked by the old town of Knaresborough.

BACKGROUND AND PLACES OF INTEREST:

Roundhay Park

One of the finest public parks in the north of England, this 700-acre park was acquired by the City of Leeds from the Nicholson family of London bankers in 1872 and was connected to the city centre in 1878 by a still-lamented electric tramway service. The Mansion House, now a restaurant, was designed by York architect John Carr. Waterloo Lake, named after the battle, was built in 1815.

Thorner

An attractive village which has kept its rural character despite being so close to Leeds. Much of the character of the village is due to the creamy-coloured Magnesian Limestone which crosses this part of Yorkshire and has resulted in the area being called 'the Yorkshire Cotswolds'.

Wetherby

A lovely old coaching and market town, on a once-important crossing of the River Wharfe, which carried the Great North Road between London and Scotland. Now thankfully bypassed by the traffic, the town's old market hall, pubs and attractive Georgian streets have both character and charm. The former railway line between Wetherby and Spofforth now forms the Harland Way walking and cycling trail.

Spofforth Castle

More a large fortified house than a castle, this extensive ruin dates from the 14th century when Henry Percy, an ancestor of Shakespeare's Hotspur, was given permission to crenellate or fortify his mansion against the threats of frequent raids by the Scots.

Knaresborough

In the lower reaches of the Nidd gorge at the edge of Knaresborough is St Robert's Cave. St Robert lived at this secluded location from 1180 to 1218. His fame spread through reported miracles and he had visits from many poor and sick people as well as King John in 1216. The cave served as a chapel, and Robert lived on the rock platform by the cave.

Below: Fields near Thorner. *Author*

Starting Point: Roundhay Park (from Leeds station see Route 1).

Finish/Return Point: Knaresborough railway station: two trains per hour to Harrogate and Leeds; hourly trains to York (MetroTrain Harrogate line).

Distance: 33km (20½ miles).

Map: OS Landranger 104 Leeds & Bradford.

Surfaces and Gradients: One steady climb of 70m; the rest of the route is undulating with short gentle climbs. Mostly minor roads and lanes; 4km (2½ miles) of smooth gravel path.

Traffic Conditions: One short section along the A661 (1km — ⅔ mile) where great care is needed.

Facilities: Cafés: Roundhay Park; several riverside cafés in Knaresborough — others also in the town centre.
Pubs: Thorner, Collingham, Linton, Spofforth and Knaresborough (several).
Shops: Thorner, small grocer; variety of food stores in Knaresborough.
WCs: Roundhay Park (above café by Waterloo Lake), Knaresborough riverside.

ROUTE INSTRUCTIONS:
From Roundhay Park South Exit (Wetherby Road) take Wetherby Road left towards the A58 and Wetherby. Turn left at the junction and follow the A58 for a short distance up the hill before taking the next right (caution!). Take the next left and go up the hill to the roundabout on the hilltop.

Turn left to Monkswood Gate and the ring road (caution!). Use the split road crossing to cross to the street opposite. Go along Ringwood Drive to the end. Turn right and go along the straight, crossing over Coal Road until the road ends at a T-junction. Turn left to Thorner.

There is a long descent into Thorner — follow the road until you reach the centre, with shops and pubs either side of the road. Continue past the church to the junction with Milner Lane, which turns off straight ahead as the road bends sharply right.

The lane follows a shallow valley before

Below: Crossroads near Thorner. *Author*

climbing up to a junction; continue straight ahead — after 1km (²/₃ mile) you pass Hetchell Wood Nature Reserve. Turn right at the next junction, then next left, signposted Collingham; ignore the forks off to the left and right as the road runs down and up a gentle dip. With views opening up, the lane meets a T-junction as it descends. Turn right to go downhill into Collingham (caution, steep bend!).

Just before the end of the road turn left and, at the end of the street, cross over the A58 by the Old Star Inn. Go straight ahead to the bridge on the A659, turn left then immediately right into Station Lane. From Station Lane take the right bend, called Beck Lane, which ends on Linton Road.

Follow this road through to Linton and Wetherby. Turn right at the next T-junction after 200m; a blue cycleway sign on the right marks the start of the route to Spofforth (car park also signed on the left). Go through the car park and turn right to go through the gate on to the path. Go under the bridge and take the left fork, through a

Above: Leeds Civic Hall. *Author*

deep wooded cutting. After ¹/₂km (¹/₄ mile) the Wetherby branch joins from the right. Continue straight ahead on the track which runs for another 4km (2¹/₂ miles).

In Spofforth join the street which leads up to the A661. Turn right on to the A661 (caution: busy with heavy lorries!). Continue along the A661 (at the bend, for Spofforth Castle keep ahead and at the sharp right turn along the lane; return to the A661) through the village and down across a stream (1km [c¹/₂ mile]) to the junction past the bridge. Take the lane leading off straight ahead. (Caution: take great care here as the traffic comes from various directions.)

Go up the hillock before the lane sweeps across open fields with very gentle contours to Little Ribston. Turn left along the B6164 and follow it for the next 4km (2¹/₂ miles) into Knaresborough — traffic is light but caution is needed at the roundabout junctions with the A658. Go straight ahead

Above: Shambles, Wetherby.
Colin Speakman

through the roundabouts to descend to the River Nidd — the bridge is controlled by traffic lights. Take the immediate left after the bridge, Abbey Road.

Abbey Road is 'access only' for traffic and makes a wonderful approach to Knaresborough. The entrance to St Robert's Cave is 50m along the riverside. Continue along Abbey Road, crossing the B6163 to continue by the river and under the cliffs to arrive in town by the riverside cafés and boats. Continue under the railway bridge and turn left up the steeply cobbled street to reach the railway station and town centre beyond.

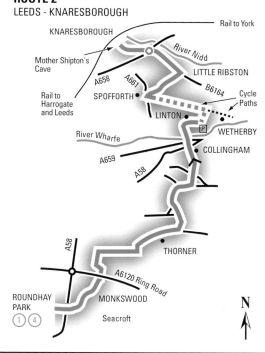

ROUTE 2
LEEDS - KNARESBOROUGH

Rail to York

KNARESBOROUGH

River Nidd

Mother Shipton's Cave

LITTLE RIBSTON

A658 A661 B6164

Cycle Paths

Rail to Harrogate and Leeds SPOFFORTH

LINTON

River Wharfe

P WETHERBY

COLLINGHAM

A659

A58

THORNER

A58

A6120 Ring Road

ROUNDHAY PARK
① ④

MONKSWOOD

Seacroft

N

LOTHERTON HALL AND SELBY ABBEY: CROSS GATES (LEEDS) TO SELBY

A ride through the gentle limestone hills east of Leeds, passing the fine country house of Lotherton Hall with its gardens and aviary. The route then winds across the Vale of York, running along the lowest reaches of the River Wharfe before it merges with the Ouse, to the old port of Selby.

BACKGROUND AND PLACES OF INTEREST:

Barwick in Elmet
This village was once an important settlement in the centre of the ancient kingdom of Elmet — an independent Celtic territory which flourished in the 7th century close to what is now modern Leeds. An earthwork behind the town's main street may have been part of the royal palace. There is a splendid maypole in the village centre which is decorated annually.

Aberford
A lovely old coaching town full of old inns (although many are no longer used as such) once serving hundreds of stage coach travellers on the Great North Road — the A1 that now bypasses the town. The Swan Inn is one which has kept its stable yards and much of its character. The village also has some interesting neo-Gothic almshouses and the remains of a windmill.

Lotherton Hall
Once the home of Sir Alvary Gascoigne (1893-1970), former British Ambassador to Japan, Russia and China, this lovely Edwardian house and its exquisite gardens has not only the Gascoigne collection of paintings, furniture and ceramics (many collected by the ambassador during his period of duty in the Far East) but also displays major Leeds City collections. There are woodland walks, a bird garden and a tea room in the old stables. It is open daily.

Towton
The little village of Towton and nearby Cock Beck was, on Palm Sunday 1461, during the Wars of the Roses, the setting for one of the bloodiest battles in English history. An estimated 20,000 men were reputed to have died, including many peers of the realm, and such was the carnage, it is said that the waters of the Cock Beck ran red with blood.

Selby
Selby is an ancient port, dating back to Anglian times. The three swans of the town's coat of arms reflect an ancient legend of Benedict, a monk from Auxerre in France who, when travelling to York in 1069 on a boat up the River Ouse, saw three beautiful swans alight on the riverbank. He took it as a sign from God to found his great abbey here, close to a small river settlement of Anglian fishermen and farmers. The magnificent abbey church remains, constructed of limestone from Monk Fryston which was brought here by a specially constructed canal from the Ouse. Modern Selby is a bustling market town — an agricultural and industrial centre on an important road and rail crossing of the Ouse.

Above Left & Right: Leeds, at the start of the route, offers a wide range of shops.
Leeds City Council

Below Left: Selby Abbey. *Peter Waller*

Starting Point: Cross Gates railway station. Frequent trains from Halifax, Bradford, Leeds, Selby and York call here (MetroTrain York and Selby line).

Cut-off Point: Ulleskelf: infrequent trains to Leeds and York.

Finish/Return Point: Selby. There are frequent trains to Leeds, Bradford and Halifax and an hourly service to York and Hull.

Distance: 36km (22 miles).

Maps: OS Landranger 104 Leeds & Bradford; 105 York & Selby.

Surfaces and Gradients: Easy rolling terrain with one short steep climb (Cross Gates-Scholes), otherwise flat. Surface: tarmac

lanes and roads with one section of cycle track (Cross Gates-Scholes).

Traffic Conditions: Quiet lanes, apart from steady traffic on 1km (²/₃ mile) section of the A162; busy traffic in Selby.

Facilities: Cafés: Lotherton Hall and Selby. Pubs: Barwick in Elmet, Aberford, Towton, Ulleskelf, Ryther, Cawood, Wistow and Selby.
Shops: Cross Gates, Barwick, Aberford and Selby.
WCs: Lotherton Hall.

ROUTE INSTRUCTIONS:
From Cross Gates station turn left and take the concrete path left, just past the electrical store. This leads on to Kennerleigh Drive. Turn left at the junction and follow it to the end. Turn left on to the next junction.

Turn left here on to Austhorpe Lane. After crossing over the railway, turn right on to Manston Lane. Passing various factories the lane soon leaves the city, running parallel to the railway.

ROUTE 3
CROSS GATES - LOTHERTON HALL - SELBY

Take the next left which is blocked off to traffic by a metal barrier and follow this lane which soon becomes a track and ascends a wooded slope. After levelling out, another metal barrier is passed where another track is met; continue straight ahead to the road. Turn right and head through Barwick in Elmet, taking the Aberford road.

The road runs across a shallow valley before ending in Aberford. Turn left and next right to go under the A1 and after 1km (²/₃ mile) the lane meets the B1217 at Lotherton Hall. From Lotherton Hall take the B1217 towards Towton (if going from the grounds of the Hall, turn left at the exit

Top: Lotherton Hall grounds.
Leeds City Council

then right on to the B1217). The road descends into the shallow valley of Cock Beck before regaining height, passing a stone cross and dropping into Towton. Turn left on to the A162 for 1km (²/₃ mile), then turn right on to the B1223 to descend on to the flat base of the plain, crossing the railway as you approach Ulleskelf.

From Ulleskelf continue along the B1223 through the villages of Ryther, Cawood and Wistow to reach Selby. Follow the signs for the town centre and the station.

LOWER WHARFEDALE: LEEDS (ROUNDHAY PARK) TO ECCUP AND ILKLEY

A ride through the northern suburbs of Leeds into surprisingly fine countryside close to the city where Airedale merges into Wharfedale. The route takes in the old Dales market town of Otley, always popular with cyclists, then the winding route north of the Wharfe, via Weston and Askwith, on the edge of Nidderdale an Area of Outstanding Natural Beauty (AONB) to the moorland resort of Ilkley.

BACKGROUND AND PLACES OF INTEREST:

Eccup
The quiet, unspoiled nature of this village, which is still largely a farming community, owes much to the existence of the reservoir which has in fact restricted the development of Leeds into this rural area, which now enjoys the protection of Green Belt status. The village pub (food available) welcomes cyclists.

The Wharfedale Viaduct
This hugely impressive stone viaduct carrying the busy Leeds-Harrogate railway dominates the Lower Wharfe Valley. It was built in 1846/7 as part of the Leeds-Thirsk Railway, is 479yd (around 430m) in length with 21 arches and 50,000 tonnes of stone were used to build it.

Otley
This fascinating old market town, overshadowed by the steep wooded hillside of Otley Chevin (now a Forest Park), has a cobbled market place and many quiet courts and alleyways. In the parish churchyard extension is a unique memorial — a model of the nearby Bramhope Tunnel and the 23 men who died in its building during the 1840s. There is also a pleasant riverside area with gardens, and a popular cyclists' café close by.

Ilkley
Superbly situated within Wharfedale in a great bowl of hills, this ancient former spa town lies on the site of a Roman fort and ford over the River Wharfe. The church has three rare Anglo-Viking crosses, and the history of the town is told in the excellent museum (open daily except Mondays) in the old Manor House, next door to the parish church. Other attractions include a good choice of cafés and pubs, an attractive riverside area, and the celebrated Ilkley Moor, with its historic White Wells spring (now a small visitor centre) high on the moor edge.

Below: The Grove, Ilkley. *Author*

Above: Cow and Calf Rocks, Ilkley Moor. *Author*

Above Right: New Inn, Eccup. *Colin Speakman*

Starting Point: Roundhay Park, Leeds (for directions from central Leeds see Route 1).

Finish/Return Point: Ilkley railway station. Frequent MetroTrain (Wharfedale line) services from Leeds and Bradford, Forster Square.

Distance: 33km (20½ miles).

Maps: OS Landranger 104 Leeds & Bradford

Surfaces and Gradients: Low hills with some steep sections as well as easy valley floor stretches; total climbing: 150m.

Traffic Conditions: Generally quiet, but some busy sections, especially along the A659 between Arthington, Pool and Otley, where care is required.

Facilities: Cafés: Roundhay Park, Otley and Ilkley.
Pubs: Roundhay Park, Eccup (to north of village), Pool, Otley, Askwith and Ilkley.
WCs: Roundhay Park, Otley and Ilkley town centre.

ROUTE INSTRUCTIONS:
From the south entrance of Roundhay Park follow the road up the slope to the Manor House, taking the road at the back of the house to Princes Avenue. Take the next right on to Park View Crescent, and turn right at the next junction. Follow Park Lane down to the traffic lights at the ring road.

Go straight ahead up Roundhay Park Lane and continue through the traffic lights at the top of the hill. Take the next left, Wigton Lane. After 1km (²/₃ mile) turn right on to Manor House Lane. The lane descends before crossing the A61 (caution, busy road!); take the reservoir road down to Eccup Reservoir.

Follow the road across the reservoir, round to the edge of Eccup village. After the farm buildings take the right fork, and turn right at the next junction. A short ascent leads to the watershed. The road drops steeply; take the left fork down, which later rises up a steep little slope. At the junction turn left as the lane runs to the valley floor and joins the A659.

Turn left on to the A659 and continue through Arthington to Pool. At Pool turn right and then left to continue on the A659 to Otley. Turn right at the traffic lights and cross the River Wharfe. The road climbs a little. Take the left turn for Askwith and go

up to Weston before going through the
attractive village of Askwith. Then (with
fine views across to Denton Hall on the
right) the road returns to the riverside for
the final stretch into Ilkley. Continue by the
playing fields until the road meets a
crossroads. Turn left to cross the river, go
straight ahead uphill to the traffic lights by
the church, cross into Brook Street and at
the top turn left for the station.

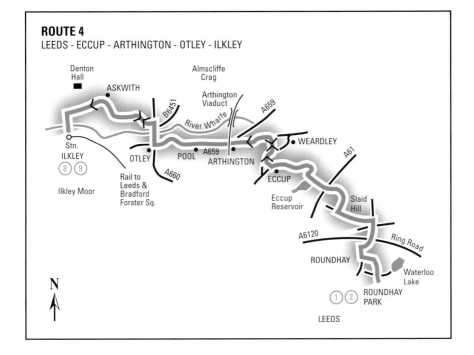

ROUTE 4
LEEDS - ECCUP - ARTHINGTON - OTLEY - ILKLEY

WESTERN DALES: GIGGLESWICK TO INGLETON AND CLAPHAM

A ride through the rolling countryside of Yorkshire's far west, between the gritstone moors of the Forest of Bowland and the limestone country of the high Western Dales dominated by the peak of Ingleborough. There are spectacular views throughout. This route runs along the edge of the Bowland Moors with wide views across the Wenning Valley to Ingleborough and later the Lune Valley. Straying a few miles into Lancashire, the route drops into Wennington before heading northeast to the village of Ingleton. A mid-level route back gives wide views in the other direction, as the route skirts the foot of Ingleborough heading down to Clapham village and then the station (2km [1½ miles] further).

BACKGROUND AND PLACES OF INTEREST:

Ingleton
A popular tourist village, dominated by a huge, disused railway viaduct. The nearby twin valleys of the Rivers Doe and Twiss offer one of the most spectacular and geologically interesting waterfall walks in the British Isles. It is worth leaving your bike at the car park to enjoy the 7km (4½-mile) walk around these famous falls, which requires at least two hours.

White Scar Cave
An impressive show cave in the Dales, about 1km (⅔ mile) along the Hawes road.

Clapham
One of the loveliest villages in the Yorkshire Dales, set in the little Clapdale Valley on either side of a stream. As well as a choice of cafés and a pub, there is a National Park Centre with interpretative displays and local information. The station platform (2km [1¼ miles] from the village) gives impressive views of the Bowland Fells. Ingleborough Cave is nearby (40 minutes' walk past the lake).

Starting Point: Giggleswick railway station (Settle station is an alternative, 2km [1¼ miles] further). Four services per day from Leeds, Skipton and Lancaster (no service to Giggleswick on winter Sunday mornings — use Settle as an alternative). NB: There is a high step down on to the platform at Giggleswick — you may need assistance.

Cut-off Point: Wennington railway station.

Finish/Return Point: Clapham railway station. Four services daily to Leeds, Skipton and Lancaster.

Distance: 41km (25 miles).

Maps: OS Landranger 98 Wensleydale & Wharfedale, 97 Lancaster & Kendal.

Surfaces and Gradients: Low undulating hills and quiet valleys. Tarmac lanes throughout.

Traffic Conditions: Light, but take extreme care crossing the very busy A65 with fast-moving traffic.

Facilities: Cafés: Ingleton, Clapham.
Pubs: Ingleton, Clapham and Clapham station.
Shops: Ingleton and Clapham.
WCs: Ingleton and Clapham.

Left: Old signpost, near Bentham. *Author*

Above: Clapham railway station. *Author*

ROUTE INSTRUCTIONS:
From Giggleswick station take the footpath exit at the top end of the car park, following the sloping path down to the road junction. Take the road on the right, under the railway bridge. The lane climbs a little. Ignore the turn-off, and then cross the railway.

Turn left at the crossroads and follow the road to Eldroth, a small hamlet. Go through

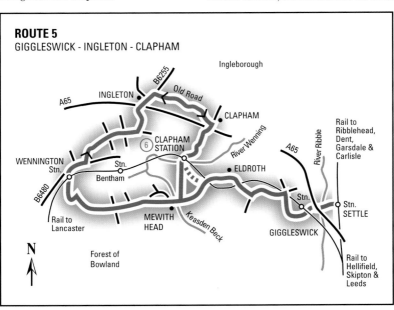

ROUTE 5
GIGGLESWICK - INGLETON - CLAPHAM

Above: Giggleswick School Chapel. *Peter Waller*

the hamlet, until the road descends steeply to cross a stream and runs under the railway again. Follow the Bentham road which ascends to rough open pasture. At the crossroads go straight ahead, over the stream and up to Mewith Head where the road is gated. Ignore the turn-off for Bentham and continue straight ahead toward Wray. At the crossroads go straight ahead again, and take the second right.

This narrow lane leads to a T-junction; turn left then right, signed for Wennington. Follow the lane which descends by Wennington station to the hamlet of Wennington. Turn left on to the main road; at the junction continue toward Settle/Bentham. Take the second left and ascend the hill, continuing until the crossroads . Go straight across, and continue straight ahead at the next crossroads for a better route into Ingleton. Follow this narrow lane until it reaches a T-junction, then go down into Ingleton. Go straight across the A65 (care required!)

then turn left and right into the village centre.

Continue through the village and on to the road signed for Hawes. Turn left at the junction and take the next right, the Old Road. This lane climbs steadily past Yarlsber, Cold Cotes and Newby Cote with a panorama of the Bowland Fells opposite. The lane descends more steeply into Clapham village. Just outside the village ignore the turn-off, and at the next junction go left into the village centre.

For Clapham station turn right at the crossroads by the post office, following the stream down. Cross the A65 Clapham bypass (caution — the cattle creep/ underpass to the left is recommended) and continue along the lane down to the station. (If you wish to return to Giggleswick — 11km [7 miles] go under the bridge and then left at the next junction back to Eldroth.)

WESTERN DALES: RIBBLEHEAD STATION THROUGH DENTDALE AND KINGSDALE

This route, the highest of the rides, runs through some of the most spectacular scenery in the Yorkshire Dales National Park (though Dentdale is officially in Cumbria). The route starts at Ribblehead, by the famous viaduct, and climbs across wild, open moorland before dropping into the dramatically beautiful Dentdale, with superb views of the Settle-Carlisle railway. Calling in at the village of Dent, the route takes a punishing climb out of Deepdale to the long, almost geometrically-shaped, valley of Kingsdale before rising over the edge to Thornton and Ingleton. A final run along the foot of Ingleborough takes the cyclist into the pretty village of Clapham.

BACKGROUND AND PLACES OF INTEREST:

Ribblehead

This station enjoys one of the wildest and highest locations of any railway station in England, in the heart of the Three Peaks. A small interpretative centre is being developed in the main station buildings on the southbound platform. The famous Ribblehead Viaduct with its 24 stone arches (the highest is over 50m [165ft] high) is a major landmark. It took four years to build, between 1870 and 1874, and during its construction a large navvy encampment grew up in the area, outlines of which, with the lines of small industrial tramways, can still be seen around nearby Batty Moss.

Denthead

Another spectacular viaduct, this time built of locally quarried black Dent Marble, a form of dark limestone. Though it has only 10 spans, these are in fact even higher, at 197ft or 64m, than Ribblehead. The next 11-arch viaduct at Arten Gill is equally impressive. In this lovely section of the Dale, where the narrow lane shares the valley with the infant River Dee, you past Dentdale Youth Hostel and the Sportsman's Inn.

Dent

One of the most beautiful of all the Dales villages, Dent was once a bustling small town. As the centre of the hand-knitting industry, its inhabitants earned the nickname 'The Terrible Knitters of Dent'. Its narrow, cobbled main street and huddle of knitters' cottages remain virtually unchanged. It was also the birthplace of Professor Adam Sedgwick (1785-1873), the great Victorian geologist who for 55 years was Woodwardian Professor of Geology at Cambridge University. A large granite fountain commemorates his long life and many charitable connections with his native village.

Kingsdale

One of the lesser known of the Yorkshire Dales, squeezing its way between the massive slopes of Whernside and Gragareth, two of the highest peaks in the Dales, this is in fact a splendid example of a deeply glaciated valley. The hills on each side have impressive limestone scars and areas of limestone pavements. This is also an area famous for its potholes and many caves.

Ingleton and Clapham (see Route 5)

Below: Dent village. *Author*

Starting Point: Ribblehead railway station on the Leeds-Settle-Carlisle line. Trains are two-hourly, less frequent on Sundays.

Finish/Return Point: Clapham railway station on the Leeds-Skipton-Lancaster line — four trains per day. (Return tickets to Ribblehead are usually accepted by Northern Spirit on the return trip from Clapham.)

Distance: 42km (26 miles).

Map: OS Landranger 98 Wensleydale & Wharfedale.

Surfaces and Gradients: Very hilly: one extremely steep climb from Deepdale and two steep descents; total climbing: 580m. Surface: tarmac lanes throughout.

Traffic Conditions: Variable traffic (can be a steady flow of tourist traffic) on the first 3km (c2 miles) from Ribblehead; otherwise quiet lanes throughout. Gated road between Dentdale and Kingsdale.

Facilities: Cafés: Dent, Ingleton and Clapham.
Pubs: Ribblehead, Denthead, Dent, Thornton, Ingleton, Clapham and Clapham station.
Shops: Dent, Ingleton and Clapham.
WCs: Dent, Ingleton and Clapham.
Youth Hostels: Dentdale (tel: 015396 25251), Ingleton (tel: 015242 41444).

ROUTE INSTRUCTIONS:
From Ribblehead station go down the station track to the road. Turn right at the Station Inn along the B6255, and at the nearby junction keep on this road in the direction of Hawes. The road climbs steadily northeastwards. Turn left on to the Dent road which soon descends steeply into Dentdale, going under Dent Head Viaduct.

The road runs along the valley floor following the river Dee downstream. Take the next left at Cowgill, crossing the river to take the narrower back lane route to Dent village.

From Dent village retrace your route for 1km (²/₃ mile), then turn right on to the Ingleton road. Climb steadily through Deepdale, the lane ascending ever more steeply through the high gated pass between the high fells of Whernside and Gragareth (for most people walking is advised!). The lane descends into Kingsdale, then passes Thornton Force as it ascends again. Continue straight ahead at the next junction to Thornton in Lonsdale, and take the next left to drop into Ingleton. Follow the road over the river into the village, turning left after the bridge to go up into the village centre.

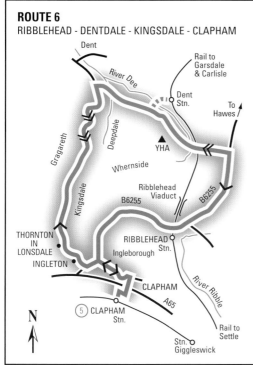

ROUTE 6
RIBBLEHEAD - DENTDALE - KINGSDALE - CLAPHAM

Dent
Rail to
Garsdale
& Carlisle
River Dee
Dent
Stn.
To
Hawes
Gragareth
Deepdale
▲
YHA
Whernside
Kingsdale
Ribblehead
Viaduct
B6255
B6255
THORNTON
IN
LONSDALE
RIBBLEHEAD
Stn.
INGLETON
Ingleborough
CLAPHAM
River Ribble
A65
N
⑤ CLAPHAM
Stn.
Rail to
Settle
Stn.
Giggleswick

Above: River Dee, Upper Dentdale.
Colin Speakman

Bottom Left: Ribblehead Viaduct.
Author

Continue through the village and on to the road signed for Hawes. Turn left at the junction and take the next lane right, the Old Road. This lane climbs steadily past Yarlsber, Cold Cotes and Newby Cote with a panorama of the Bowland Fells opposite. The lane descends more steeply into Clapham village. Just outside the village ignore the turn-off and at the next junction go left into the village centre. For Clapham station turn right at the crossroads by the post office, following the stream down. Cross the A65 Clapham bypass (caution, the A65 is very busy) and continue along the lane down to the station.

NORTHERN DALES: GARSDALE TO NORTHALLERTON VIA RICHMOND

This is the longest and most challenging of the rides — a full day is needed. The route starts from the high point of Garsdale station on the famous Settle-Carlisle railway, near the source of the Ure. It runs down Wensleydale taking in the town of Hawes and the attractive villages of Askrigg, Carperby and Redmire, then follows a shelf overlooking the main valley and the smaller dales of Coverdale and Bishopdale before climbing steeply by Castle Bolton to the open heather moors and dropping into Lower Swaledale. The route then follows the thickly wooded slopes by the River Swale before running into Richmond. Descending from Richmond into the northern end of the Vale of York,

the route's final section winds from the River Swale southeastwards across the rich rolling farmland and woods into the county town of Northallerton. The hilliest part of the route is in the middle section between Carperby and Swaledale. If time allows, don't fail to visit the spectacular Aysgarth Falls, and Richmond is also worth a stopover. As an alternative, you might wish to break the ride into two parts, taking more time to see the many attractions on the route. The Youth Hostel at Aysgarth Falls is about halfway on the route.

BACKGROUND AND PLACES OF INTEREST:

Hawes

A busy Dales market town with a good choice of shops, pubs and cafés. Market day is Tuesday. Of outstanding interest is the Dales Countryside Museum in the old station yard (open daily in summer months, weekends only in winter; also contains the National Park Information Centre) and the Hawes Creamery, home of the famous Wensleydale Cheese, where you can see cheese being made and which also has a shop with cheese on sale, and a café. The

Hawes Rope Works in the station yard, where you can watch specialised rope being made, is also of exceptional interest.

Hardraw Force
One of the most spectacular waterfalls in the Dales, in a deep gorge behind the Green Dragon Inn (small entrance fee payable), which is used for regular brass band contests.

Askrigg
A small former market town which is the fictional Darrowby of the James Herriot television series. Once the centre of the Dales clockmaking industry, there are many 17th and 18th century buildings, plus a cobbled market area and fine medieval church.

Castle Bolton
This massive 14th century castle (open to visitors daily, with a museum) — where Mary, Queen of Scots was imprisoned — lies in a magnificent setting, close to a village of great charm.

Richmond
The magnificent Norman castle on a cliff above the River Swale still dominates the market town that grew around its ramparts to service its needs. Richmond, with its winding alleyways and cobbled courts, keeps much of its medieval atmosphere and charm, and also boasts a fine Georgian area with elegant houses and one of the country's finest Georgian theatres — still used for theatrical performances. There is a small museum in the town square.

Northallerton
Though it is the county town of England's largest county, North Yorkshire, with an imposing County Hall, Northallerton is little more than an extended, linear village. There are, however, some interesting yards and courts, pleasant shops and pubs, and a choice of cafés.

Left: Wheatsheaf Inn, Carperby, Wensleydale.
Author

Starting Point: Garsdale railway station on the Settle-Carlisle line. Two-hourly train service between Leeds, Settle and Carlisle — 3/4 trains a day on Sundays.

Finish/Return Point: Northallerton railway station. Hourly train service to York and Leeds (Trans-Pennine).

Distance: 77km (48 miles).

Maps: OS Landranger 98 Wensleydale & Wharfedale, 92 Barnard Castle, 99 Northallerton & Ripon.

Surfaces and Gradients: Fairly hilly, mostly in the middle section; total climb 250-300m.

Traffic Conditions: Light traffic apart from Richmond to Brompton-on-Swale section, which will require extra care.

Facilities: Cafés: Hawes, Aysgarth Falls and Richmond.
Pubs: Garsdale Head, Hawes, Askrigg, Richmond, Yafforth and Northallerton.
Shops: Hawes, Askrigg, Richmond and Northallerton.
WCs: Garsdale station, Hawes, Aysgarth Falls and Richmond.
Youth Hostels: Hawes (tel: 01969 667368), Aysgarth Falls (tel: 01969 663260) and Grinton Lodge (tel: 01748 884206).

ROUTE INSTRUCTIONS:
From Garsdale station turn right to go down the hill to the A684. Turn right and continue along this road to Hawes. In Hawes follow the main street down and turn left (signed Hardraw) to cross the river towards the next junction. If visiting Hardraw Force (behind the Green Dragon Inn) turn left here. Otherwise, turn right at the junction and follow this lane through to Carperby.

Turn left for Castle Bolton, go up the steep climb, then follow the narrow lane as it dips to cross a small beck. At the crossroads take the gated lane straight ahead (note a small blue cycle sticker on a post).

Where the lane ends at a junction, turn left and climb steeply up Redmire Scar. The

Left: Richmond, near the riverside. *Author*

Right: Castle Bolton, Wensleydale. *Author*

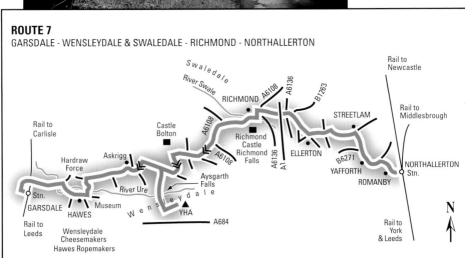

ROUTE 7
GARSDALE - WENSLEYDALE & SWALEDALE - RICHMOND - NORTHALLERTON

road levels out on Leyburn Moor and passes the firing ranges. Part way along, the road is joined by the A6108. Turn off left on to the A6108 after 1km (²/₃ mile) and follow it as far as Richmond.

In Richmond, for the market place, dismount at the first roundabout and take the third turning; there is a cycle stand in the market place. The riverside and castle are signed from the market place.

To continue, from the first roundabout take the 'All routes' turning and go straight ahead over the next roundabout. After the traffic lights, turn right for Brompton-on-Swale; the road descends to the river valley. Take the left fork to pass under the A1 and soon after go straight across the A6136.

(Caution, this road is very busy!) Turn right at next junction to take the B6271 and go through Bolton-on-Swale. Take the next left, signed for Whitwell, and follow this narrow lane through fields and woodland, going straight ahead at the crossroads to Streetlam. Turn right and go back on to the B6271. Go through Yafforth and take the next right by the golf course to Romanby.

In Romanby turn left on to the main road and go over the level crossing, then take the right fork into Northallerton. Turn right to go to the station car park — this is the easiest entrance to approach. Use the underpass for southbound trains. Northallerton town centre is about half a mile away — turn left at the main road.

WASHBURNDALE: ILKLEY TO KNARESBOROUGH

This is a fairly challenging but rewarding ride through Yorkshire's 'Little Lake District', the Washburn Valley, with stiff climbs by heather moors and thrilling descents. There are spectacular views across Washburndale and back across Wharfedale before you pass the outskirts of Harrogate to reach the lovely old town of Knaresborough on the River Nidd, with its castle and spectacular riverside scenery.

BACKGROUND AND PLACES OF INTEREST:

Ilkley
Ilkley lies in mid-Wharfedale, on the edge of the West Yorkshire conurbation and the Yorkshire Dales. This former spa town, with its many fine stone houses and shops, known as the 'Heather Spa' or the 'Malvern of the North', was famous in Victorian times for the quality of its pure air and the hydropathic treatment using springs from nearby Ilkley Moor. It is also the subject of the famous 'Baht 'at' folk song. It remains a popular place for excursions, with fashionable shops and wine bars. Its good public transport makes it an excellent centre for walkers and cyclists, with its wide choice of riverside and moorland walks and rides.

Washburndale
During the late 19th and early 20th century, most of the valley of the little River Washburn, a tributary of the Wharfe, was flooded to create fresh water supplies for the growing city of Leeds. The great reservoirs of Lindley, Swinsty and Fewston and surrounding woodland have long been a popular area of recreation for Leeds people, and now form part of the Nidderdale Area of Outstanding Natural Beauty.

Timble
This tiny village, with its well-known Timble Inn — a popular place for both walkers and cyclists (food is usually available) — has remained remarkably unspoiled, despite being so close to Leeds.

Knaresborough
Far older than its neighbour Harrogate, Knaresborough was an important medieval market town, though it is now overshadowed by its larger neighbour. As well as its dramatically situated cliff-top castle and handsome, much photographed, Victorian railway viaduct, Knaresborough has lovely riverside walks (with popular cyclists' cafés), a busy market place with shops and a weekly market, as well as the so-called Petrifying Well, in which lime-rich waters appear to calcify hats and gloves placed in the dripping waters of a grotto.

Below: Ilkley Manor House. *Colin Speakman*

Starting Point: Ilkley railway station. Frequent MetroTrain Wharfedale line services from Leeds and Bradford, Forster Square to Ilkley. Day Rover ticket is valid to Ilkley.

Finish/Return Point: Knaresborough railway station. Hourly services from Knaresborough to Leeds (Harrogate line) and York. Day Rover ticket is valid between Leeds and Horsforth only.

Distance: 40km (25 miles).

Map: OS Landranger 104 Leeds & Bradford.

Surfaces and Gradients: First half is hilly with two climbs, one of 200m (650ft), the other 90m (300ft). After the moors of Washburndale, there is a long gentle descent into the rolling countryside around Harrogate and Knaresborough.

Traffic Conditions: Light traffic on quiet back roads throughout — some care needed in Ilkley and at junctions with main roads.

Facilities: Cafés: Ilkley and Knaresborough. Pubs: Ilkley, Askwith, Timble, Bland Hill (Fewston), Beckwithshaw and Follifoot. Shops: Ilkley and Knaresborough.

WCs: Ilkley, Knaresborough and Fewston Reservoir/Swinsty.

ROUTE INSTRUCTIONS:

From Ilkley station turn right and walk (rather than negotiate a rather awkward junction) to the pavement right down on Brook Street to cross at the zebra crossing. Follow Brook Street down to the traffic lights and continue straight ahead over the River Wharfe.

Take the first right, and continue along for 5km (c3 miles) (until you reach Askwith village. Turn left; the road climbs steadily (ignore the next turn-off on the left). At the T-junction at the summit, turn left (caution, some trucks use this hilly route) and the road runs along the top of the moor before descending a 12% gradient.

Take the first right (signed Timble) and where the road bends sharp left, continue ahead for Timble hamlet. After Timble the narrow lane rejoins the main lane which then crosses Fewston Reservoir.

After the reservoir, take the first left (ignore the turn-offs just after this point) as the lane makes a short steep climb. Go straight ahead at the next crossroads; the road then dips and climbs to the B6451. Turn right and continue for 1km ($^2/_3$ mile) and soon after the Sun Inn take the narrow

ROUTE 8
ILKLEY- KNARESBOROUGH VIA WASHBURNDALE

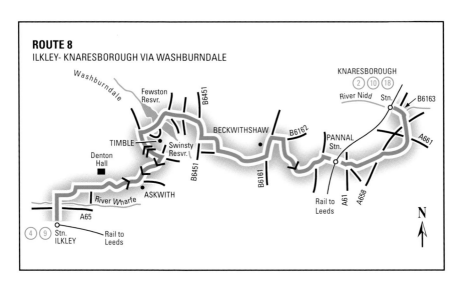

lane on the left. Follow this lane to the end, and turn left again, where the road runs along the plateau of Sandwith Moor before reaching the summit. From here a long gentle descent begins.

The road meets the B6161; turn left into Beckwithshaw and take the second right. After 0.5km (¼ mile), turn right, taking the lane for Burn Bridge. Keep on this lane ignoring turn-offs, and beware of a narrow and very tight bend just before Burn Bridge (signed 10%, speed limit 15mph).

At the mini-roundabout turn left, then right at the second roundabout; follow this street to the end and turn right to pass over a stream and Pannal station. Cross over the A61 (take care!), and take the left-hand road which leads over a hillock to Follifoot.

Just as the road ends, take the tarmac path exactly opposite — between the roadsigns. This crosses the bypass road and leads to a gap in a fence controlled by

barriers. Continue to Follifoot by turning right at the next junction.

Go through Follifoot and continue along the road until it meets the A661. Turn left on to the A661 — after a few metres take the closed road on the right, marked by metal gates. This road is a traffic-free bridlepath and leads up to the B6163 (take care crossing the bypass!) which descends to Knaresborough's riverside. Go over the bridge and turn immediately left along the riverside for cafés, boats, etc.

Knaresborough station is at the top of the steep, cobbled lane to the right before the viaduct (walking advised!), reached via a level crossing.

Top: Swinsty Reservoir, Fewston, Washburndale. *Author*

Right: Bolton Abbey, Wharfedale. *Author*

SOUTHERN DALES: MALHAMDALE AND WHARFEDALE TO ILKLEY

A route through the south of the Yorkshire Dales National Park, taking quiet lanes from Hellifield across the lower part of Malhamdale and into Wharfedale, before following this most beautiful of dales past the picturesque villages of Thorpe, Grassington, Appletreewick and Bolton Abbey to Ilkley.

BACKGROUND AND PLACES OF INTEREST:

Hellifield Station
This grand, canopied station was once a major junction where the Lancashire & Yorkshire Railway (from Manchester via Clitheroe) and the Midland Railway (from Leeds via Skipton) met en route to Carlisle. Elaborate waiting and refreshment rooms were provided for passengers awaiting connections to and from the Scottish expresses. The station has now been restored and a café opened, and there are ambitious schemes to develop the station into a major railway heritage centre and base for steam operations along the Settle-Carlisle line.

Winterburn Hall
A superb example of a Tudor yeoman's house. No public access.

Thorpe
Known as Thorpe in the Hollow or the Hidden Village, this is one of the loveliest and least spoiled villages in the Yorkshire Dales. No facilities for visitors.

Grassington
By contrast, Grassington is a bustling tourist centre, a former lead mining village clustered around a delightful cobbled square with narrow courts leading off, containing a choice of pubs, cafés and shops, mostly angled at the thousands of visitors who come here every weekend. It is an excellent centre for local walks and cycle rides in superb countryside. The National Park Visitor Centre in the main car park on Hebden Road has interpretative displays and a range of local information. There are toilets close by.

Appletreewick
Another delightful village with two inns, and two cottages which date from Tudor times. The village once hosted a regular Onion Fair.

Bolton Priory and Strid Woods
One of the most beautiful monastic ruins in England, at a superb riverside location, Bolton Priory is just one of the many delights of this beautiful estate, with a choice of woodland and riverside walks, including the awe-inspiring and highly dangerous 2m-wide Strid chasm which carries the full flow of the River Wharfe. The Cavendish Pavilion, just across the wooden bridge, offers a wide range of refreshments, from ice cream and light snacks to full meals. Cyclists are welcome, as they are at Buffers farmhouse, high above the valley on the lane at Storiths, which also serves a range of refreshments.

Starting Point: Hellifield railway station. Trains leave about every two hours, from Leeds, Skipton, Settle and Lancaster (Settle-Carlisle and Leeds-Morecambe lines). Sundays have a less frequent service.

Finish/Return Point: Ilkley railway station. There are trains every 30 minutes to Leeds and Bradford; hourly on Sundays.

Distance: 47km (29 miles).

Maps: OS Landranger 103 Blackburn & Burnley, 98 Wensleydale & Wharfedale (both areas covered by 1:25,000 Outdoor Leisure 10 Yorkshire Dales: Southern Area) and 104 Leeds & Bradford.

Surfaces and Gradients: Tarmac lanes throughout.

Traffic Conditions: Mostly quiet lanes, although traffic gets busier near Grassington and Bolton Abbey, especially on Sunday afternoons.

Facilities: Cafés: Hellifield station, Grassington, Hebden and Cavendish Pavilion (Strid Woods — north of Bolton Abbey), Storiths and Ilkley.
Pubs: Hellifield, Airton, Hetton, Cracoe, Grassington, Appletreewick and Bolton Bridge.
Shops: Hellifield, Grassington, Hebden and Ilkley.

Above: Bolton Bridge, Wharfedale. *Author*

Right: Grassington Square. *Colin Speakman*

WCs: Linton Falls, Grassington, Hebden, Bolton Abbey and Ilkley.

ROUTE INSTRUCTIONS:
From Hellifield station drive turn left on to the A65 and go through Hellifield towards Skipton. Take the left fork, a narrow lane which crosses the railway and winds its way to the hamlet of Otterburn. Go straight ahead to Airton, then straight ahead at the crossroads in the village centre. Crossing over the River Aire, the lane climbs, following the Yorkshire Dales cycleway round the base of the hills to Winterburn.

At the bridge turn left to pass Winterburn Hall and ascend gradually toward Hetton. Turn left to go through the village and drop down the hill to the junction. Take the Cracoe road (ignore the Bordley turn-off), which crosses the railway, before joining the B6265. Turn left on to the road (caution, traffic can speed along here!) and continue through Cracoe. Where the B6265 bends left, continue straight ahead on the narrow lane. This climbs by the conical limestone hills (reef knolls) below Thorpe Fell. Turn left (right to Thorpe) to drop down to the B6160. Continue to the next crossroads then turn right downhill to Linton Falls; at small bridge (the Falls are straight ahead) take the road left to pass by Threshfield School, to emerge at Grassington Bridge. Cross the river and go up the hill to Grassington Square.

From Grassington take the B6265 eastward to Hebden. In Hebden turn right just before the bridge, going through the village to follow Hebden Beck down towards the River Wharfe, then go up along the side of the main valley. Passing the village of Burnsall across the river opposite (superb views), turn right at the next junction to drop down to another T-junction. Turn left here to go through Appletreewick, then right at the next junction towards Howgill.

This road loses height to cross Fir Beck before climbing again under the lower wooded slopes of Simon Seat. Dropping height near Barden Bridge, take the left fork to keep height as the lane runs above the Strid and drops down by the Strid Woods entrance. Cross over the wooden bridge and take the road out to the main road. Turn left to go though Bolton Abbey and continue through to Bolton Bridge.

Turn left after the Devonshire Arms pub to take the old bridge over the river, and cross the A59 (caution!) for Beamsley. Follow this narrow lane as it climbs up into the hamlet of Beamsley before dropping near the river again. There is another climb through Nesfield, before the road drops down past Ilkley golf course and enters Ilkley. Continue as far as the crossroads, then turn right to cross over the River Wharfe once again, climbing uphill. At the traffic lights go straight ahead up Brook Street; the station is left from the top junction.

ROUTE 9
HELLIFIELD - GRASSINGTON - ILKLEY

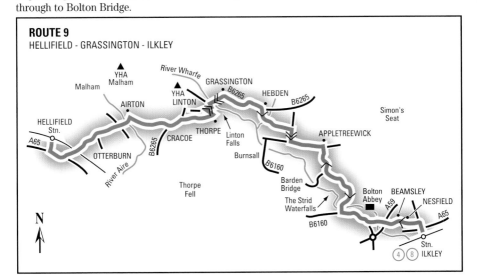

ROUTE 10

THE EASTERN DALES: KNARESBOROUGH AND KIRKBY MALZEARD CIRCULAR

A circular ride through the Nidderdale Area of Outstanding Natural Beauty along the back lanes of the Pennine foothills, crossing the quiet valleys on the eastern fringe of the Yorkshire Dales. The route passes by magnificent monuments such as Fountains Abbey and Ripon Cathedral and the long medieval village of Kirkby Malzeard. Once in Ripon, the route runs along the edge of the Vale of York, passing great estates set in fine parkland before rising gently through the rich farmland back to Knaresborough.

BACKGROUND AND PLACES OF INTEREST:

Knaresborough (see Routes 2 and 8)

Fountains Abbey
One of the finest Cistercian ruins in Europe, Fountains Abbey dates from the 12th century when a small band of monks, escaping from what they saw as the dissolute life in their parent abbey in York, were given land beside the little River Skell. By the 16th century it was, because of the wool trade, one of the richest and most powerful monastic settlements in England. After the Dissolution it eventually came into the hands of John Aislabie, Chancellor of

the Exchequer, who, when he retired after the South Sea Bubble scandal, landscaped the Studley Royal estate with extensive water gardens and a deer park, creating what is now a World Heritage Site owned and managed by the National Trust. It is open daily — there are tea rooms at the main entrances.

Kirkby Malzeard
Once an important medieval market town, Kirkby Malzeard is situated on a network of roads from Coverdale and Nidderdale which literally led to the market. Though this long, attractive village is no longer such an important centre, it hosts the Fountains Dairy cheese factory, renowned for its high quality local Dales cheeses.

Ripon
One of England's smallest cities, Ripon owes its origins to monks from Melrose Abbey who around 673 established a small church by the confluence of the Rivers Ure and Skell. Only part of the Saxon crypt survives today, most of the fine cathedral above it being built between 1154 and 1530 in a variety of Gothic styles. The town that grew around it has a charter which goes back to the time of King Alfred in AD886, and in later years Ripon flourished as a market town and small manufacturing centre. The Wakeman, or Watchman, of Ripon still blows his horn (the town's symbol) at 9pm every night at each corner of the fine cobbled market place. The half-timbered 14th century Wakeman's House is now a small museum.

Start and Finish Point: Knaresborough railway station. There is an hourly rail service from Leeds, Harrogate and York.

Distance: 53km (33 miles).

Map: OS Landranger 99 Northallerton & Ripon.

Surfaces and Gradients: Hilly in parts

between Ripley and Kirkby Malzeard; downhill to Ripon; flat in the Ripon area; undulating near Knaresborough.

Traffic Conditions: The first 6km (4 miles) along the B6165 are fairly busy. The rest quiet.

Facilities: Cafés/Tea Rooms: Knaresborough, Ripley, Fountains Abbey, Kirkby Malzeard

Above: Classical temple at Fountains Abbey. *Author*

Right: Littlethorpe church front, near Ripon. *Author*

and Ripon.
Pubs: Knaresborough, Ripley, Winksley and Kirkby Malzeard.
Shops: Knaresborough, Ripley, Kirkby Malzeard and Ripon.
Youth Hostel: Ellingstring (near Masham), tel: 01677 460216.

ROUTE INSTRUCTIONS:
From Knaresborough railway station start at the York-bound side of the station; from the level crossing head towards the path marked by a large metal gate and a gap. Take this path past the church entrance and turn right, cross the church gardens then join a short street which ends at traffic lights. Cross straight ahead.

The next section is on the B6165, which can be busy, although gradients are easy and cycling is not unpleasant. After 6km (4 miles) cross the roundabout (take care, busy traffic on the A61!) to go into Ripley village.

Top: Cyclists on Dallowgill Moors, near Kirkby Malzeard. *Colin Speakman*

Above: Copgrove Hall. *Author*

From Ripley continue to the second roundabout and turn left to take the B6165. After about 1km (²/₃ mile) turn right; the road is signed as the route for Fountains Abbey. The road climbs steadily before levelling out.

Continue for about 3km (1³/₄ miles), passing a crossroads and at the second junction turn right, down Watergate Road (signed for Fountains Village). The road descends a short steep slope before rising again by a hilltop ruined tower, which is protected by the National Trust and is accessible by foot from the road. The lane dips again to Fountains Abbey; keep descending on the lane to pass the abbey's old entrance.

With tight, hairpin bends the lane runs over the River Skell and climbs up past the new official entrance to Fountains Abbey. Continue straight ahead passing Aldfield until the lane reaches the B6265. Turn left and then immediately right on to a very narrow lane marked with a 6ft 6in restriction. The lane descends and meets another lane: turn right. A further descent leads to the River Laver, followed by a short stiff climb up to Winksley. Go straight through Winksley (beware any oncoming traffic on this narrow lane). The lane meets a wider back road which leads to Kirkby Malzeard and is well signed.

As you reach the village turn left to find the shops along the main street. Return to

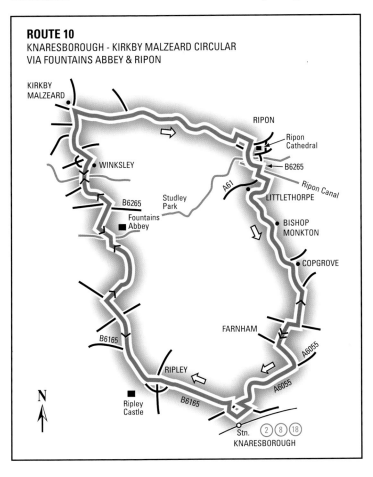

ROUTE 10
KNARESBOROUGH - KIRKBY MALZEARD CIRCULAR
VIA FOUNTAINS ABBEY & RIPON

KIRKBY MALZEARD

RIPON

Ripon Cathedral

WINKSLEY

B6265

B6265

Studley Park

Ripon Canal

LITTLETHORPE

A61

Fountains Abbey

BISHOP MONKTON

COPGROVE

FARNHAM

B6165

A6055

RIPLEY

A6055

N

Ripley Castle

B6165

Stn. ②⑧⑱
KNARESBOROUGH

take the Ripon road (straight ahead from the main street) — an easy 10km (6 miles) away and which is well signed. As you approach Ripon take the road signed for the city centre, which forks off left. Turn right when you reach the centre and follow the road to the market place — turn left to go to the bus station. At the edge of the bus station (near the supermarket) is a cycle park, and a short footpath (dismount) to Ripon Cathedral.

From Ripon Cathedral either turn right to go down the slope and turn left on to the B6265. Continue until just before the roundabout and cross over the road to take the canal towpath under the roundabout junction.

Or (for a pleasant back lane route out), turn left on to the brick road round the cathedral, then after the bend turn right down Residence Lane. At the end of the lane turn right then fork left at the triangle junction, bending right to take the road marked by a warning sign for a ford. Cross over the footbridge and continue right. Cross the B6265, go right and then up the shallow embankment to join the canal path

before turning left. Follow this path under the main roundabout junction.

Cross over the canal by means of the bridge and turn left on to the Littlethorpe road. Continue for about 1½km (1 mile) then turn left on to the lane signed for Bishop Monkton. From here the lanes are signed for Knaresborough, but make sure you turn right just after the village sign for Copgrove.

After Copgrove, the road dips and ends after a sharp bend; turn right. With a gradual climb the road ends at a crossroads on the hilltop; take the one-way route signed for Knaresborough straight ahead. This narrow lane soon descends quite steeply and ends at a T-junction; go left from here and after 1km (⅔ mile) follow the A6055 for the last stretch into Knaresborough. At the main junction in Knaresborough the easiest route is to turn left and go up the slope before turning down Station Lane (which is just before the pelican crossing) to the railway station.

Below: Cottages by Fountains Abbey entrance. *Author*

Holderness is the name of the area of low-lying countryside which extends along the north bank of the Humber through East Riding as far as Spurn Point. This route runs through the small villages of South Holderness near the estuary of the Humber. There are wide open views across the estuary allowing you to watch ships on their way up to the Humber ports. Inland the flat expanse of the diked open fields gives the landscape a feel of the Netherlands.

The return section of this route follows the South Holderness Rail Trail, which at the time of writing is in a poor state, particularly after wet weather. Check on the current state of the trail with East Riding Council (telephone number is at the end of the book). Currently it is rideable from Ottringham, although proper mountain bikes are needed to cover more of the trail starting nearer Patrington.

BACKGROUND AND PLACES OF INTEREST:

Hull

This large international port has in recent years enjoyed something of a renaissance as a tourist centre, with extensive redevelopment of former dockland areas into marinas, with cafés, wine bars, boutiques and themed restaurants. If you have time, the celebrated Maritime (Docks) Museum, Hull Transport Museum and the Wilberforce Museum in the city centre are not to be missed.

Hedon

Once an important medieval port, Hedon is an ancient borough with a splendid church, a magnificent Jacobean town hall, and a rare collection of silver including the oldest civic mace (1415) of any town in England. In the garden of Holyrood House is to be found the Kilnsea Cross, said to have been erected at Ravenser to commemorate the landing of Henry Bolingbroke (later Henry IV) in 1399. The site was eventually destroyed by coastal erosion and the cross

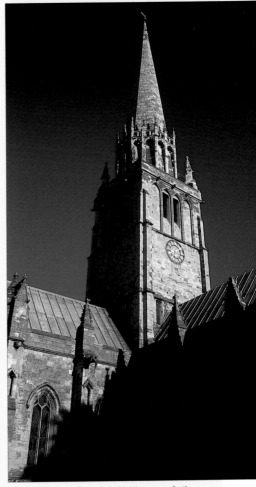

Above: Patrington church, Holderness. *Author*

washed up on the beach at Kilnsea in 1818.

Paull

An extraordinary coastal village containing a small harbour with a lighthouse (built in 1836), a number of interesting houses and cottages, and a fine medieval (Perpendicular) church.

Sunk Island

This area of Holderness was once in the River Humber, but emerged as an island as surrounding river deposits were drained and reclaimed as highly productive farmland.

Patrington

St Patrick's Church at Patrington with its tall spire visible as you ride towards the village is a notable Holderness landmark. Known as 'The Queen of Holderness', it is reputed to be the most beautiful parish church in England. It was built between 1310 and 1349 in the Decorated style, and its spire is 189ft (about 60m) high. The village, which has pubs and cafés, is a good point to break a journey.

The South Holderness Rail Trail

The Hull to Withernsea railway line was closed in 1964 but was converted during the 1980s by Humberside County Council into the South Holderness Rail Trail — a walking and cycling route from Hull to Patrington and Winestead. There are sections which need attention, so look out for local information.

Starting Point: Hull railway station. Hourly services from Leeds. Regular Trans-Pennine services from York, Doncaster and Sheffield — booking is advisable.

Distance: 65km (67km avoiding the Rail Trail [40/42 miles]).

Maps: OS Landranger 107 Kingston Upon Hull, 113 Grimsby.

Surfaces and Gradients: Flat gradient. Tarmac lanes, rough track and path on Withernsea Rail Trail.

Traffic Conditions: On-road bike lane through Hull, then traffic-calmed streets — the signed part of the National Cycle Route. 1. Traffic-free along the Rail Trail; the lanes through Paull, Stone Creek and Sunk Island are very quiet. The A1033 is not very busy near Patrington, but some cars speed so take care at all times.

Facilities: Cafés: Hull and Patrington (tea shop closes 2.30pm; chip shop).
Pubs: Hull, Hedon, Paull, Patrington Haven and Patrington.
Shops: Hull and Patrington.
WCs: Hull and Patrington.

Above: Boats moored at Stone Creek. *Author*

Right: Mudflats at Stone Creek leading to the Humber estuary, with Grimsby in the background. *Author*

ROUTE INSTRUCTIONS:

From Hull station turn right on to Ferensway and take the next left. Follow this road straight ahead as it becomes a bike/bus route only. At the end turn right on to Alfred Gelder Street and continue straight ahead past the traffic lights, over the bridge and straight across again at the next junction. After about 100m turn right down Wilson Street then left past the Blacksmith's Arms pub and continue straight ahead over the next junction. After the road turns a corner turn right to take the bike lane over the main road (traffic control lights provided).

Go straight ahead following the road under the rail bridge. Turn right on to Belmont Street following the NCR signs round Escourt Street and turn right near the main road on to the recreation ground. The route meets the old railbed by the bridge; turn left on to the Withernsea Rail Trail.

The trail passes the outer estates of Hull before crossing open fields. After a bridge the trail is crossed by a minor road. Turn right to go to Hedon village. Follow this

Left: View from Paull Holme across the Humber to Immingham. *Author*

Right: The road out of Stone Creek. *Author*

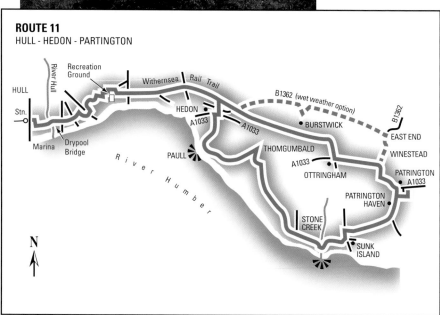

ROUTE 11
HULL - HEDON - PARTINGTON

HULL

River Hull

Stn.

Recreation Ground

Withernsea Rail Trail

HEDON

A1033

A1033

B1362 (wet weather option)

B1362

BURSTWICK

EAST END

WINESTEAD

Marina

Drypool Bridge

PAULL

THOMGUMBALD

A1033

OTTRINGHAM

PATRINGTON

A1033

PATRINGTON HAVEN

River Humber

STONE CREEK

SUNK ISLAND

N

one-way road straight across the crossroads to the main road. Turn right and take the next left to Paull.

As Paull is approached, take the right fork to pass by the estuary shore and the viewpoint. Turn right at the next junction to the edge of Thorngumbald. At the crossroads turn right on to the lane signed Stone Creek.

Go past New House Farm; the road ahead is signed as a dead end but it is still passable for cyclists. Continue along to Stone Creek — a couple of houses where a small stream reaches the estuary. Near Stone Creek the tarmac lane gives way to a rough track where it crosses the creek. The tarmac soon returns and leads straight on to the tiny hamlet of Sunk Island.

At Sunk Island crossroads turn left then take the next right for Patrington.

Approaching the village of Patrington, take the third turn left to go round the church. Turn left at the next junction to get to the village centre at the old market place.

From the market place go straight ahead on to the A1033 towards Hull (caution, traffic tends to speed along this road!). If you wish to return via the Withernsea Rail Trail (assuming the trail surface has been improved, or the weather has been dry) turn off right at Ottringham. Follow the lane for just over 1km (²/₃ mile) to where the line crosses the lane, marked by old wooden gates, and turn left on to the trail. Near

Keyingham, 2km (1¼ miles) further on, there is a diversion round the grounds of some houses. Turn right, take the next left on to a track, then turn left back on to the trail. Follow the trail back through the edge of Hedon to Hull.

However, if you need to avoid this part of the trail from Patrington follow the A1033 for 2km (1¼ miles) then turn right on the corner (caution!) to Winestead, continue to the B1362, turn left and continue to Hedon. As you enter Hedon take the Rail Trail which crosses the road, and go back towards Hull.

EAST YORKSHIRE WOLDS: MALTON TO HUNMANBY

A ride along the rolling Wolds to Hunmanby Gap, with a quiet beach and wide views along the coastline. The terrain is easy despite the climbs and good views are possible on a clear day. The ride starts at the twin villages of Malton and Norton, soon leaving the Derwent Valley with a climb out of Settrington up Thorpe Bassett Wold and a long descent down the gentle slope of the Wolds. After threading a way through small villages surrounded by arable fields, an easy climb leads to Hunmanby and the relatively secluded Hunmanby Gap. Hunmanby Gap offers a fine beach with views along the eroding coastline to Filey and Bempton Cliffs.

BACKGROUND AND PLACES OF INTEREST:

Malton

A former inland port on the once-navigable River Derwent, Malton, with its warehouses and dockside areas, is an important and busy market town and local centre, serving a large hinterland of the Wolds, Vale of Pickering and Howardian Hills. There is a small, 18th century town hall, a handsome parish church, a small museum and several old inns, including one that belongs to the local Malton brewery. St Mary's church in Old Malton is a relic of the remarkable Gilbertine Priory, founded in the 12th century by Street Gilbert, a Lincolnshire parish priest, which had both Benedictine nuns and Augustinian canons, with the church carefully partitioned for both orders to hear holy service without seeing the other. Six miles west of Malton stands Castle Howard, the magnificent baroque country house of the Howard family (for more details see Route 21).

Settrington Beacon

An ancient site for one of the chain of beacons used to carry important messages across the Yorkshire Wolds in medieval times — 199m above sea level.

West Lutton, Weaverthorpe and Wold Newton

Typical small Wolds villages, each with character and charm. Weaverthorpe has an interesting church, part of which, including the tower, is Norman.

Hunmanby

This large Wolds village also has a Norman church, an unusual early 19th century lockup for local inebriates and a pinfold, where stray sheep or cattle were rounded up until collected by their owners on payment of a small fine.

Top Left: The road approaching Hunmanby Gap.
Author

Left: Distant view of Castle Howard, near Malton at the start of the route. *Author*

Starting Point: Malton railway station. Hourly trains from Leeds, more frequent services from York and Scarborough. Every two hours trains run through from Huddersfield or Halifax and Bradford.

Finish/Return Point: Hunmanby railway station. Trains every two hours, or every hour in the afternoon to Scarborough. Services are less frequent from autumn to spring.

Distance: 34km (22 miles), including the 6km/4-mile return trip to Hunmanby Gap from Hunmanby.

Maps: OS Landranger 100 Malton & Pickering, 101 Scarborough.

Surfaces and Gradients: Easy, punctuated with short climbs totalling 290m (including 60m back from the beach).

Traffic Conditions: Some traffic in Norton, otherwise quiet throughout.

Facilities: Cafés: Malton; Hunmanby village and refreshments at Hunmanby Gap (seasonal).

Pubs: Malton, Norton, Weaverthorpe and Hunmanby village.
WCs: Malton (market place).

ROUTE INSTRUCTIONS:
From Malton station turn right then continue to the junction by the level crossing. (Caution, traffic approaches from several different directions!) Turn right on to the B1248, which bends left and runs through Norton main street. Turn right to follow the B1248 for another 1km (²/₃ mile) before turning left for Settrington up and along a miniature ridge. Continue on this lane until it ends at a T-junction.

Turn left then right, go up the slope and bend left at the junction where the road levels out, signed for West Lutton. After coasting on the ridge the lane dips to join a wider road just outside West Lutton. From now on it is a straight flat run through the villages of East Lutton, Weaverthorpe and over the B1249 to Wold Newton.

Continue through Wold Newton on the Bridlington road; where the road bends sharp right take the lane which leads off straight ahead. This lane soon climbs steadily before dropping more steeply into Hunmanby. (Caution, junction at the bottom of the hill!)

Turn right for the station; otherwise, for Hunmanby Gap, 3km (2 miles) away, turn left and take the next right (signed for Hunmanby Gap), Sands Road, which crosses over the A165 (caution crossing this road!) before dropping down into the gap.

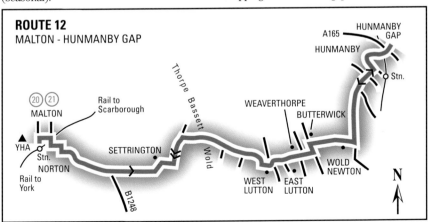

ROUTE 12
MALTON - HUNMANBY GAP

THE SOUTHERN WOLDS: BROUGH TO BEVERLEY

After leaving the Humber Estuary at Brough the route runs through the ancient settlements of South and North Cave at the foot of the Yorkshire Wolds, following the line of the Wolds and along the eastern edge of the Vale of York. North of Market Weighton the route climbs steadily by Londesborough and follows the flat top of the Wolds before following the long, gentle slope down into Middleton on the Wolds. The final section winds through the beautiful villages of Lund and Cherry Burton, before running into Beverley with its stunning minster and historic streets.

With heavy traffic in Beverley, you may find it easier to find your way to the station and park your bike there in order to explore the pedestrianised town centre on foot.

BACKGROUND AND PLACES OF INTEREST:

Beverley
One of the finest medieval and Georgian towns in England, with twin market places and over 350 buildings of historic and architectural interest, including the Georgian Guild Hall. Beverley Minster is one of the finest Gothic buildings in eastern England, originally dating from Norman times but with magnificent features from every period since. St Mary's Church is almost as impressive as the minster — this great medieval church stands at the opposite end of the town centre.

Market Weighton
An attractive, compact market town. Once an important railway junction, all the lines were closed by the Beeching axe and the former Market Weighton-Beverley line is now a cycleway and an alternative route to Beverley. It is worth making a detour 2km

Above: Stream by North Cave church. *Author*

(1¹⁄₄ miles) northeast of the town to the village of Goodmanham. According to legend, the village church is one of the earliest Christian sites in Britain, being built on the spot where in AD627 Paulinus, the Pope's emissary, converted King Edwin of Northumbria to Christianity.

Londesborough
This is a beautiful estate village, the house and park of which once belonged to the Clifford family, ancestors of the Duke of Devonshire. Later, George Hudson, the disgraced Victorian railway tycoon, built an imposing avenue from his house to his private station on the Market Weighton-York railway.

Starting Point: Brough railway station: frequent trains from Hull, and an hourly service from Selby, Leeds, Huddersfield and York.

Finish/Return Point: Beverley railway station: frequent trains (half-hourly on weekdays) to Hull and Bridlington, and hourly to Scarborough.

Distance: 54km (33½ miles).

Maps: OS Landranger 106 Market Weighton, 107 Kingston Upon Hull.

Surfaces and Gradients: One steady climb out of Market Weighton of 130m. The first section to Market Weighton is flat. A long descent after the hill to Middleton and thereafter gently undulating country lanes to Beverley. Tarmac lanes and roads throughout.

Traffic Conditions: Some traffic between Brough and the Ellerker turn off. The final approach to Beverley town centre is on a fairly busy road and extra care is needed.

Facilities: Cafés: Brough (chip shop) and Beverley. Pubs: Brough, Market Weighton, Middleton, Etton, Lund and Beverley. Shops: Brough, South

Cave, Market Weighton, Middleton and Beverley.
WCs: Market Weighton and Beverley.
Youth Hostel: Beverley Friary
— a Dominican Friary in Friar's Lane (tel: 01482 867430).

ROUTE INSTRUCTIONS:
From Brough station, exit by the road below the Hull-bound platform and turn right at the junction. At the mini-roundabout turn left up Cave Road. At the next roundabout turn left again on the road

Right: Beverley Minster.
Author

signed for South Cave. After 1½km (1 mile) turn left to Ellerker. Take the first right, Mill Hill, round into the little village. Turn right and continue to the end (the Trans-Pennine Trail turns off before here) and take the bridge over the A63 into South Cave.

Go left along the road to North Cave; turn right at the junction and again right at the next junction; just before the church turn left. Follow the narrow lane over the bridge and around the back of North Cave to the crossroads. Go straight ahead and follow this lane through South and North Cliffe to Market Weighton.

The road ends where it has been cut through and fenced off by the bypass, but you can rejoin it by turning right and following the wooden fence to its end where a concrete path leads through the fence. Continue along the street and turn left at the end; at the roundabout turn left to the town centre.

Turn right just past the zebra crossing and on to the road signed for Londesborough. The A163 is crossed at a roundabout before the road descends, then the climb round Londesborough begins. At the junction turn right up to Londesborough crossroads; continue uphill on to the lane signed Nunburnholme and Warter. At the summit bend right at the junction (signed Middleton). The lane runs above the thick woods of Londesborough along a flat ridge; ignoring the turn-offs, continue until the road turns sharply 90° and take the next turn-off right, followed by a long 5km (3-mile) descent into Middleton. Turn right into the village and cross the A163 (turn left then immediately right); go on to

the one-way street and turn left to continue to the B1248.

Turn right and take the next left for Lund. Head to the village green, and turn right by the pub to follow Lockington Road. Turn right at the next junction. Follow this lane straight along until it rises gently to join the B1248; with great care join it and take the next right (caution, traffic can be heavy and busy in this section!). Follow this lane into Etton, before turning left to Cherry Burton (signed NCR 66). At Cherry Burton turn left down through the village to the crossroads with the B1248; the NCR now turns right (caution!) on to the B1248 using a cycle path along the left side of the road. The route follows the B1248 as far as the roundabout on the edge of Beverley and then continues straight ahead along the A164 to the town centre. At the traffic lights

ROUTE 13
BROUGH - MARKET WEIGHTON - BEVERLEY

MIDDLETON ON THE WOLD
A163
LONDESBOROUGH
Londesborough Park
MARKET WEIGHTON
LUND
B1248
NORTH CLIFFE
SOUTH CLIFFE
ETTON
NORTH CAVE
B1230
CHERRY
BURTON
B1248
W
o
l
d
s
SOUTH
CAVE
A63
A164
BEVERLEY
Beverley ■
Minster
ELLERKER
Rail to
Selby, York
& Leeds
N
Stn.
BROUGH
Rail to
Hull
River Humber

Top Left: View from Londesborough Field, near Market Weighton. *Author*

Bottom Left: Londesborough Valley. *Author*

turn left for the station, turning right at the roundabout (caution, use outer lane!) to go straight ahead at the traffic lights to head to the next roundabout, and left to the station.

Left: Market Weighton church. *Author*

Below: Ellerker village, near Brough. *Author*

YORKSHIRE WOLDS AND COAST: BRIDLINGTON, RUDSTON AND FLAMBOROUGH HEAD

A route which runs through the gently rolling East Yorkshire Wolds, along the shallow valley of Gypsy Race, between the undulating fields of the Wolds and ends by the spectacular chalk cliffs and lighthouse of Flamborough Head. The wide open country of the Wolds is in contrast to the compact villages along the route.

BACKGROUND AND PLACES OF INTEREST:

Bridlington
A busy and popular seaside resort, with fine sandy beaches, cliffs and a fascinating old harbour, Bridlington retains an old village area away from the coast, and a fine old priory, founded by Augustinian canons in the 12th century. If you have time to spare before returning, it is worth exploring Sewerby Hall and Park, with its aviary, art gallery, museum and fine gardens, immediately to the north of the town (this can be accessed on the return ride by extending the route into Bridlington via Sewerby).

Rudston
In the churchyard at Rudston is a huge stone monolith, the largest standing stone in Britain, 8m (25ft) high and 2m wide. It must have been dragged here from Cayton Bay, the nearest source of similar rock, some 16km (10 miles) away. Nobody knows its origin or purpose. The church has a Norman tower.

Burton Fleming
A pretty Wolds village notable for its church which has a Norman doorway.

Bempton
It is worth following the cul-de-sac lane 2km (1¼ miles) north of the village to Bempton Cliffs, for the RSPB Reserve, one of Britain's finest seabird sanctuaries, notable for its cormorants, puffins, kittiwakes, shags, guillemots and Britain's only colony of mainland gannets. The village also has an early Victorian (1846) railway station and the remains of a windmill.

Below: Rudston monolith. *Author*

Flamborough
A pleasant coastal village with a moving memorial to victims of the coast's many storms. Flamborough Head itself offers magnificent views of the North Sea, the sea-carved cliffs and a chance to see the impressive lighthouse, which was built in 1806 by John Matson of Bridlington. There is a small Heritage Coast Information Centre in the car park.

Starting Point: Bridlington railway station. There are regular trains from Hull (Wolds Coast line), less frequent from Scarborough.

Finish/Return Point: Bempton railway station. There are trains every 2 hours to Hull, Bridlington and Scarborough; every hour in the afternoon. Services are less frequent from autumn to spring. (For a greater choice of trains continue into Bridlington via Sewerby and the coast road — 7km [4¹/₃ miles].)

Distance: 41km (25¹/₂ miles). To return to Bridlington via Sewerby add another 7km (4.5miles).

Map: OS Landranger 101 Scarborough & Bridlington.

Surfaces and Gradients: Rolling low hills; a short climb of around 40m between Bridlington and Rudston, then rising to 100m west of Bempton. Tarmac lanes throughout.

Traffic Conditions: Bridlington town and the area around the station and along the A165 can be extremely busy in the main holiday season, otherwise quiet throughout.

Facilities: Cafés: Bridlington, (including buffet at railway station), Flamborough Head and Sewerby.
Pubs: Bridlington, Burton Fleming, Bempton and Flamborough.
Shops: Bridlington, Flamborough village.
WCs: Bridlington, Flamborough Head.

ROUTE INSTRUCTIONS:
From Bridlington railway station, go down the station drive and turn left over the level crossing. At the roundabout take the second turn (signed Scarborough) and go left at the traffic lights. Turn right along South Back Lane then left at the Burton Engineering Co building.

Turn right up the one-way street to pass the edge of the old town, then left. Continue

Right: Flamborough Head cliffs. *Author*

to where the street bends right and leave the road to take a surfaced footpath by the trees and grass up to the A165. Cross over the A165 to the B1253 which starts straight ahead.

The road follows the valley of Gypsy Race with a climb around Boynton. At Rudston the standing stone is in the churchyard (signed). Continue on the same road before turning right for Burton Fleming.

For the next 3km (c2 miles) cross a flat, open stretch of countryside. Turn right at the junction before the village — you might wish to look at Burton Fleming, although the pretty village has only a pub on offer for the traveller. The road now starts a gradual ascent, broken by a dip down to a crossroads; continue straight ahead through Grindale and turn left. The gentle ascent continues; cross the A165 (caution, holiday traffic makes this road very busy!) to the lane opposite, signed for Flamborough.

The lane begins a gentle descent and runs alongside the railway before ending at a T-junction. Turn left over the level crossing and continue to the B1229. Turn left through Bempton; the road crosses Danes Dyke 2km (1¹/₂ miles) after the village before entering Flamborough village. Turn right in the village centre then take the next left (signed for South Landing and lighthouse) and follow the road to the lighthouse at the tip of Flamborough Head. Return to Flamborough village and continue towards Bridlington, as far as Marton. Where the main road bends sharply right, go instead straight ahead on the lane which bends round to Bempton railway station. To continue into Bridlington, keep straight ahead over the level crossing, and turn left at the junction following the signs to Sewerby, then left past Sewerby Church into the centre of Bridlington.

ROUTE 14
BRIDLINGTON - RUDSTON - FLAMBOROUGH HEAD - BEMPTON

Rail to Scarborough

A165

FLAMBOROUGH

BEMPTON Stn.

BURTON FLEMING

Flamborough Head

GRINDALE

MARTON

Lighthouse

A165

SEWERBY

B1253

North Sea

RUDSTON

Stn.

BRIDLINGTON Harbour

Rail to Hull

N

THE HOLME VALLEY AND THE DARK PEAK: STOCKSMOOR TO SHEPLEY

A ride that runs through the rolling hills in southwestern Yorkshire, starting in the fertile countryside around the Holme Valley, before reaching the austere and treeless landscape of the gritstone Pennines, or Dark Peak, on the edge of the Peak District National Park. The route starts in the small wooded valleys around Stocksmoor. There is a climb up to Fulstone, and a further climb takes the rider up to the high lanes above Penistone, before the route drops into the Upper Don Valley at Millhouse Green and joins the Trans-Pennine trail. The 4-mile section along the trail with its railway gradient allows the regaining of lost height with ease as the landscape quickly changes to moorland; the route runs along the northern boundary of the Peak District National Park. The final climb out of Dunford Bridge enters a landscape of high gritstone moorland and passes above Winscar Reservoir before offering spectacular views to the north across West Yorkshire. Keeping the height, the route follows the high lanes above Holmfirth before dropping down on the same track, but with a final easy descent into Shepley. If you so wish, you can retrace your route to Stocksmoor to make this route a circular.

Right: Lane between Stocksmoor and Fulstone, Kirklees. *Author*

BACKGROUND AND PLACES OF INTEREST:

The Trans-Pennine Trail /The Woodhead Line

The Trans-Pennine Trail is a planned walking, cycling and horseriding route between Hull and Liverpool, which is being opened in stages. This particular section utilises part of the Woodhead Route, a major electrified railway across the Pennines which carried heavy freight and passenger trains on the shortest route between Manchester and Sheffield, until closed because of a remarkable lack of foresight. Ironically, its tunnels were built to Continental gauge in anticipation of a Channel Tunnel rail link. The current resurgence of rail freight has led to speculation that one day this major route could be reopened, which would require the building of a new path to carry the Trans-Pennine Trail alongside the new railway.

Dunford Bridge

This tiny hamlet, on the boundary of the Peak District National Park, with just a handful of cottages, once boasted its own railway station which closed to passengers in 1970. Close by is Winscar Reservoir, one of several moorland reservoirs on the upper part of the River Don.

Starting Point: Stocksmoor railway station: hourly service between Sheffield and Huddersfield (MetroTrain Penistone line); two-hourly on Sundays.

Finish/Return Point: Shepley railway station: hourly service between Sheffield and Huddersfield; two-hourly on Sundays.

Distance: 31km (19 miles).

Map: OS Landranger 110 Sheffield & Huddersfield.

Surfaces and Gradients: Hilly, particularly in the first section, but with long level stretches; an easier climb from Dunford Bridge. Tarmac surface, but smooth gravel on Trans-Pennine Trial. Optional cycle track for last section.

Traffic Conditions: Light traffic on quiet back lanes, traffic free section along the Trans-Pennine Trail in the Upper Don Valley.

Facilities: Pubs: Cross Roads, south of Fulstone, Millhouse Green, Dunford Bridge, Victoria, Shepley and Stocksmoor (near station).
Shops: Shepley.
Youth Hostel: Langsett (tel: 0114 288 4541).

ROUTE INSTRUCTIONS:
From Stocksmoor station, turn left to go through to the edge of the village, pass the crossroads on to the Fulstone road and take the left fork as the lane descends slightly.

The lane crosses a stream and then climbs into Fulstone; turn left on to White Ley Bank. The lane bends round the hillside with wide views across the Holme Valley. Turn left at the next junction; the narrow lane crosses a stream before rising up to cross the A635. (Caution, visibility is reduced here!) Cross over to the lane opposite and go up the steep incline. After the summit the lane descends to the crossroads at Lane Head.

Go straight ahead and take the immediate right fork, Dearne Dike Road. A long, rolling section along the high pastures follows for 5km (3 miles) until the road ends at a T-junction. Left on to Royd Moor Hill, and left again to descend steeply into Millhouse Green.

Cross straight over the A628 and follow the road over the River Don, before turning sharp left where the road bends right. This narrow lane soon leads up to an old level crossing on the Trans-Pennine Trail. Turn right on to the trail, and follow it for 8km (5 miles) as far as Dunford Bridge.

Below: Millhouse Green, Upper Don Valley. *Author*

Right: Holme Valley and the surrounding moors, near Shepley. *Author*

At Dunford Bridge turn left off the track on to the road (unless you want to stop off at the pub). Turn right to cross the River Don and climb the last 100m. Turn left on to Dunford Road as the final climb gradually rises above Winscar and Harden Reservoirs. Just past the summit turn right to take the road along the hilltop; ignoring turn-offs, continue to the Victoria pub at the crossroads. Continue straight ahead until Lane Head is reached again.

(An alternative is to take the first left; turn off from the Victoria and follow this narrow lane with the views above the Holme Valley; the final section to the incline below Lane Head is a rough track.) From Lane Head turn left to return down the steep incline.

(To return to Stockmsoor, retrace your route from here across the A635 and through Fulstone.) Go down the incline to where the steepest gradient eases and turn right on to a narrow lane, partly concealed by houses. Cross the A635 (caution!) and follow the road opposite down into Shepley. At the bottom of the hill, turn left just before the main road on to Station Road. Follow this road down to the station.

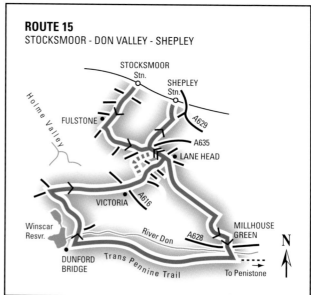

ROUTE 15
STOCKSMOOR - DON VALLEY - SHEPLEY

STOCKSMOOR
Stn.

SHEPLEY
Stn.

Holme Valley

FULSTONE

A629

A635

LANE HEAD

VICTORIA

A616

Winscar
Resvr.

River Don

A628

MILLHOUSE
GREEN

DUNFORD
BRIDGE

Trans Pennine Trail

To Penistone

N

TRANS-PENNINE TRAIL: SILKSTONE COMMON TO THE EARTH CENTRE, CONISBROUGH

A journey through the centuries as you trace South Yorkshire's industrial heritage, starting with canals and mills, then passing through an old mining landscape to finish with the newest technology present in the brand-new Earth Centre, which offers a glimpse of the future. The route starts in Silkstone Common, passes the lake of Worsbrough Country Park and then goes through the countryside near Wombwell. After Wombwell the route enters the renewed landscape of the old coalfields before following the River Dearne to Conisbrough. If you wish, you can continue along the Trans-Pennine Trail to Doncaster and beyond.

BACKGROUND AND PLACES OF INTEREST:

The Trans-Pennine Trail
The Trans-Pennine Trail is a multi-user route between Hull and Liverpool with links to and from such towns as Sheffield, Doncaster, Chesterfield, Leeds, Wakefield and Manchester. The core route runs across the heart of the Pennines and the Dark Peak. It is being opened in stages, and will form part of the National Cycle Network.

Silkstone Common
This small former mining community suffered a terrible disaster in 1838 when a violent thunderstorm caused a flood that engulfed the entrance to Moorfield colliery. Twenty-five children, boys and girls, aged between seven and 17 were drowned. A memorial to the disaster is in Silkstone churchyard.

Worsbrough Country Park
A small country park close to the Dove Valley and Trans-Pennine Trail. The main features of the park are the Worsbrough Reservoir, now a birdlife and nature

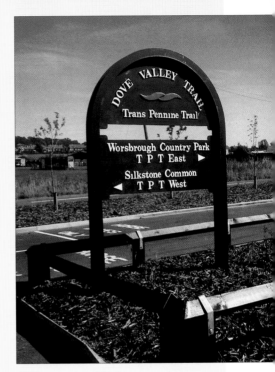

Above: Metal sign on the Trans-Pennine Trail, Worsbrough Country Park. *Author*

reserve, and the little Worsbrough Mill Museum. This 17th century water (and later steam) mill was used to grind corn, and remained in commercial use until the 1960s. It is now restored to full working order.

Conisbrough Castle
Built by Hamelin Plantagenet, half brother to King Henry II, in the 12th century, this castle with its spectacular keep provided the historical background for Sir Walter Scott's romantic novel *Ivanhoe*. It is open daily.

The Earth Centre (see Route 23)

Starting Point: Silkstone Common railway station. Hourly service from Huddersfield, Barnsley and Sheffield (Penistone line). Two-hourly on Sundays.

Cut-off Point: Bolton upon Dearne railway station. Regular trains to Sheffield, Wakefield and Leeds.

Finish/Return Point: Conisbrough railway station. There is a regular Sheffield-Doncaster-Hull service.

Distance: 28km (17 miles).

Maps: OS Landranger 110 Sheffield & Huddersfield, 111 Sheffield and Doncaster.

Surfaces and Gradients: Flat. Smooth gravel surface on most sections, but rougher on the current unofficial section (Bolton upon Dearne-Harlington).

Traffic Conditions: Most of this route is along the traffic free Trans-Pennine Trail. Care is needed in the diversion through Bolton upon Dearne.

Facilities: Cafés: Worsbrough Country Park and the Earth Centre, Coisbrough.
Pubs: Silkstone Common, Bolton upon Dearne and Harlington.
Stores: Silkstone Common and Bolton upon Dearne.
WCs: Worsbrough Country Park and the Earth Centre, Conisbrough.

ROUTE INSTRUCTIONS:
From Silkstone Common station go down to the road and turn left, then immediately right (in front of the newsagent). Follow this lane down and, just before the bridge, turn off left on to the Trans-Pennine Trail (TPT).

The trail crosses over the M1; continue along the trail and cross a minor road after 1km (²/₃ mile), near a small car park. Shortly afterwards a path leads off from the right to Worsbrough Country Park. To go to the Park and Museum, dismount and follow this path along the lake edge then take the bridge to the other side, turning left to the Visitor Centre. Otherwise, continue along the TPT to follow this route.

At Tinsley Aldham junction bend right to follow the TPT and go over the two bridges; the TPT then bends right. Go over the minor road entering the redevelopment area and follow the newest section of the TPT. The trail goes under the Broomhill roundabout and through a shallow cutting. Take the track that climbs off left which then skirts

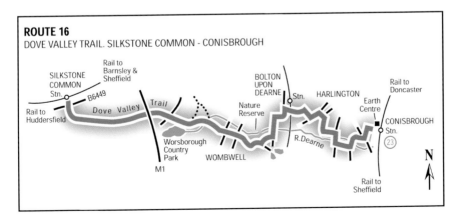

Top Left: Trans-Pennine Trail, near Silkstone Common. *Author*

Above: Winscar Reservoir, near the source of the River Don. *Author*

Above Right: Sculpture on the Trans-Pennine Trail, near Silkstone. *Author*

along the edge of a nature reserve and follows the River Dearne. Where there is a junction of tracks by a bridge continue straight ahead; the path narrows before emerging by a road. Turn left on to the road and over the bridge by the Bolton upon Dearne town signs. Follow the road into the village, taking great care by the roundabout where the priority of traffic is unclear. Turn right and continue to Bolton upon Dearne station.

From the station entrance continue along the street where it soon becomes a rough track; follow this track to the edge of Harlington. Turn left on to the road into

Harlington then right on to Doncaster Road, turning right on to Mill Lane soon after. The TPT begins again, following the river downstream. This leads to a wooden bridge across the river, before crossing a road. Go straight ahead and follow the surfaced track as it winds round relandscaped land and makes a short ascent. Cross the lane (which leads to the council depot) and the entrance to the Earth Centre soon appears on the right.

Descend the slope for the Earth Centre, and Conisbrough railway station is by the main road entrance, just over the river bridge.

ROUTE 16
DOVE VALLEY TRAIL. SILKSTONE COMMON - CONISBROUGH

SILKSTONE COMMON Stn.

Rail to Barnsley & Sheffield

B6449

Rail to Huddersfield

Dove Valley Trail

Worsborough Country Park

M1

WOMBWELL

Nature Reserve

BOLTON UPON DEARNE

Stn.

R.Dearne

HARLINGTON

Earth Centre

Rail to Doncaster

CONISBROUGH Stn.

(23)

Rail to Sheffield

N

A SOUTH PENNINES TRAVERSE: SOWERBY BRIDGE, HAWORTH AND KEIGHLEY

This ride through the South Pennines offers contrasting industrial and rural landscapes. It begins with a steep climb out of Calderdale which soon rewards the rider with spectacular moorland views. The route then crosses steeply undulating countryside around the Brontë moors and the popular village of Haworth before dropping down into the busy town of Keighley in the Aire Valley.

Above: Sowerby Bridge. *Author*

BACKGROUND AND PLACES OF INTEREST:

Sowerby Bridge

Once a major woollen manufacturing centre, which rapidly moved from the hilltop weaving village of Sowerby to the canal and railway-served valley bottom, Sowerby Bridge is still dominated by fine mill buildings, grouped around the River Calder and the Rochdale Canal.

Oxenhope

A moorland mill village which has not changed its character. This is the southern terminus of the Keighley & Worth Valley Railway, and the location of the railway's main engine shed museum, with a number of historic locomotives and some interesting memorabilia. The celebrated film *The Railway Children* was made on this line, which operates preserved steam and diesel services every weekend all year and daily during the main school holiday periods. There are special events on certain weekends.
(For information tel: 01535 647777.)

Haworth

This world-famous literary village was the home of the three remarkable Brontë sisters, Charlotte, Emily and Anne, together with their ill-fated brother, Branwell. Their books still bring visitors from all over the world both to Haworth and to the surrounding moorland described in their books. Despite the millions of visitors, cafés and many souvenir shops, the village with its steep cobbled streets has not changed its character. The Parsonage Museum, where the authors lived all their adult lives, is well worth visiting, and there is an excellent, well stocked Tourist Information Centre at the top of the village.

Oakworth

It is worth taking time to explore Holden Park, on the left-hand side as you ride through this mill village towards Keighley. This is a small, unusual little public park with elaborate stone grottoes around a bowling green, and a strange triumphal arch — the whole comprising an atmospheric Victorian folly.

Keighley

A busy manufacturing town and shopping centre, with pleasant pedestrianised central areas, an old church, busy shopping arcades and a choice of pubs and cafés. It is the northern terminus of the Worth Valley Railway (café on the station bridge).

Above: Luddenden Dean from Mount Tabor.

Starting Point: Sowerby Bridge railway station. Frequent trains from Halifax, Bradford Interchange, Leeds and York on the MetroTrain Caldervale line.

Finish/Return Point: Keighley railway station. Trains every 30 minutes to both Leeds and Bradford Forster Square (MetroTrain Airedale line — Metro Day Rover valid). The route can be shortened by taking the steam train from Oxenhope or Haworth to Keighley on the Keighley & Worth Valley Railway (Metro Day Rover not valid). For times and details see the MetroTrain timetable.

Distance: 31km (19 miles).

Map: OS Landranger 104 Leeds & Bradford.

Surfaces and Gradients: Tarmac lanes and roads throughout except for a short cobbled potholed section on Ovenden Moor and cobblestones in Haworth. Climbs total around 590m, including 355m from Sowerby Bridge to Ovenden Moor.

Traffic Conditions: Care is needed on the slopes as the lanes can be very narrow and visibility is restricted. Traffic is busy in Keighley town centre, but the route keeps main road riding to a minimum.

Facilities: Cafés: Sowerby Bridge, Oxenhope (Worth Valley Railway), Haworth and Keighley.
Pubs: Sowerby Bridge, Mount Tabor, Withens (Ovenden Moor), Oxenhope, Haworth, Oakworth and Keighley.
Shops: Sowerby Bridge, Oxenhope, Haworth, Oakworth and Keighley.
WCs: Oxenhope station, Haworth and Keighley.
Youth Hostel: Haworth (Lees Lane, on the Oakworth side of Haworth, tel: 01535 642234).

ROUTE INSTRUCTIONS:
From Sowerby Bridge station take Station Road down to the T-junction. Turn right under the rail bridge and cross over the River Calder. Take the first left — a narrow lane which soon starts to climb up and over the Rochdale Canal. At Hill Top turn left then right, up a steep hill which leads to the main road. (Caution — the road is narrow and steep!)

At the main road turn right then take the first left. This road climbs steadily; follow it round two sharp bends before turning off left, up Green Hill, where it meets a wider road. Continue straight ahead. Ignore the turn-offs at the next junction and continue ahead — Mount Tabor is signed 1 mile distant. A panorama across Luddenden Dean opens up on the left and where the road forks take the right — Heath Hill Road. The road dips slightly to enter Mount Tabor and views eastward and southward over Halifax and beyond (to the Vale of York, Emley Moor transmitter) appear. Turn left at next junction (signed Wainstalls), to face Luddenden Dean again. Turn right at next fork which is signed 'Withens', with the green rosette of the West Yorkshire Cycleway.

This middle part of the route follows the West Yorkshire Cycleway until Stanbury, so the green rosette signs (which are not at all of the junctions) can help with navigation. The final ascent to Ovenden Moor is steady and not too steep, the wind farm on Ovenden Moor making a powerful landmark. Withens pub is passed just before the summit, before reaching Warley Moor Reservoir. Views open up to the north; on a clear day you can see into the Yorkshire Dales as far as Pen-y-ghent and Ingleborough. Along the summit the road becomes more of a track for about 1km (²/₃ mile), before regaining its surface for the steep descent into Oxenhope.

Just above Oxenhope turn right on to the main road into the village and descend to the crossroads; turn left to go down past the station. Go right at the junction and up the hill to the next junction, then right again into Haworth, up the cobbled Main Street. Take the left fork at the information centre and, where West Lane is met, turn left for Stanbury.

Again there is a steep and narrow descent to cross a stream before climbing into Stanbury; then once again go down to cross the River Worth before taking a short rise up the other side. Turn sharp right on to Oldfield Lane, which rises gradually, and panoramic views of the Worth Valley across to Ovenden Moor appear. At the Harehills Lane/Hob Cote Lane junction turn right to Oakworth.

A steep descent takes you into Oakworth, then go left at the Golden Fleece pub and left again up Griffe View. Bend right at the top to go to the roundabout and continue straight ahead towards Gooseye. However, on the descent turn right for Keighley.

A long descent into Keighley town centre follows, joining the Haworth road to continue into town. Just past the roundabout use the pelican crossing to cross to the pedestrianised area. Bend right here to join a road and turn right past Keighley market. Turn left at the traffic lights to follow the main road to the station (go straight ahead at the next junction). The station is on the right — it may be necessary to use the pelican crossing to reach the station.

ROUTE 17
SOWERBY BRIDGE - HAWORTH - KEIGHLEY

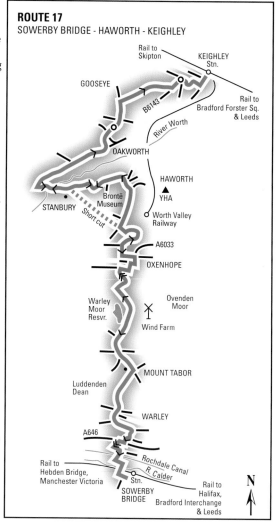

ACROSS THE VALE OF YORK: YORK TO KNARESBOROUGH

A ride across the gentle countryside of the Vale of York, linking two of Yorkshire's most popular tourist destinations: the historic city of York and the beautiful old town of Knaresborough. As well as a number of pleasant villages, this ride takes in the fine National Trust property of Beningbrough Hall (well worth a visit, so avoid doing this ride on a Thursday or a Friday when the house and park are closed), then through unspoiled deep rural countryside by quiet villages and using a network of quiet lanes.

BACKGROUND AND PLACES OF INTEREST:

York (see Route 1)

Beningbrough Hall and Gardens
A fine Georgian mansion, owned by the National Trust. Dating from 1716, it contains one of the most impressive baroque interiors in England, richly decorated with wood carving and with a magnificent collection of pictures, including many on loan from the National Portrait Gallery. There is a fully equipped Victorian laundry, extensive grounds including a new walled garden and refreshment facilities. It is open daily (except Thursdays and Fridays) between 11am and 5pm, from the end of March to the end of October. For further information tel: 01904 470666.

Knaresborough (see Routes 2 and 8)

Below: Seat made from recycled farm machinery on the Sustrans route north of York. *Author*

Starting Point: York railway station (or the riverside in York, see Route 1). There are frequent trains from Leeds and Huddersfield (MetroTrain York and Selby line), regular services from Harrogate and Knaresborough (Harrogate line), and also services from Hull, Selby and Scarborough.

Finish/Return Point: Knaresborough railway station: two trains per hour to Leeds and hourly trains to York (MetroTrain Harrogate line).

Distance: 35km (22 miles).

Maps: OS Landranger York 105, 100 Malton & Pickering, 99 Northallerton & Ripon, 104 Leeds & Bradford (optional).

Surfaces and Gradients: The route is flat as far as Great Ouseburn, with some gentle climbs thereafter. It follows tarmac lanes and minor roads, with a section of cycle path on smooth gravel. Bikes need to be lifted up the steps to cross the River Ouse in York.

Traffic Conditions: The route is generally on quiet lanes with a section on the traffic-free Sustrans bike path. The last stretch on the A6055 into Knaresborough has some traffic.

Right: Beningbrough Hall. *Peter Waller*

Below: York Minster. *Frederick Penford*

ROUTE 18
YORK - KNARESBOROUGH

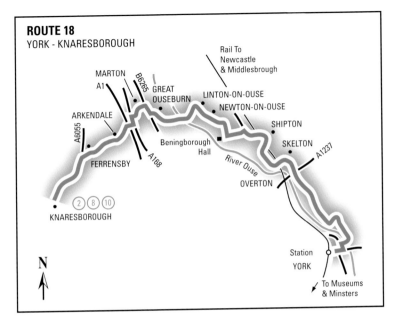

Facilities: Cafés: York and Beningbrough Hall (see below). There are several riverside cafés in Knaresborough and others in the town centre.
Pubs: York (wide choice!), Newton-on-Ouse, Linton-on-Ouse, Great Ouseburn, Arkendale and Knaresborough.
Shops: York and Knaresborough; general store at Linton-on-Ouse.
WCs: York and Knaresborough.

ROUTE INSTRUCTIONS:

From York railway station turn left and take the first left at the traffic lights. Just before the railway bridge turn right at the traffic island to turn on to the path which leads on to the banks of the River Ouse. Cross over the river using the steps.

This section of the route follows the York-Beningbrough cycle path, and is well signed as it runs northward along the banks of the River Ouse. Where the path meets the York northern bypass, turn left to go under the bridge. At Rawcliffe Farm the cycle path appears to end by a gate, but turn left and go through another gate where the path rejoins the riverside and winds through a little wood before meeting Beningbrough

Lane — signed as National Cycle Route (NCR) 65. Beningbrough Hall and Park (National Trust) is on the left.

For the next few kilometres follow NCR 65; the route crosses under the main London-Scotland railway, passes the hamlet of Overton then goes over the railway. Turn left, following NCR 65, to cross the railway once again at the edge of Shipton. NCR 65 passes Beningbrough Hall using a very narrow lane to Newton-on-Ouse. Just before Linton-on-Ouse Route 65 turns off right; instead continue straight ahead to go through Linton-on-Ouse.

After 2½km (1½ miles) turn left and cross the river at Aldwark toll bridge. At the next junction turn right to go through Great Ouseburn and Branton Green to meet the B6265. Turn right then take the next left to pass below Marton. The lane ends at the A168 feeder road for the A1; turn left to follow it until the next junction. Turn right to go through Arkendale, ignoring the turn-offs, to join the A6055 at Ferrensby. From here it is just under 4km (2½ miles) to Knaresborough. Turn left at the main junction, and on the slope turn right to go down Station Road for the station.

ROUTE 19

THE ESK VALLEY: CASTLETON TO WHITBY

The little River Esk carves its way through a dramatic, steep valley in the northern part of the North York Moors National Park, sharing its valley with the scenic Esk Valley railway line (Middlesbrough to Whitby) and a network of minor, sometimes steep, country lanes, terminating in the spectacular old whaling port and seaside resort of Whitby.

BACKGROUND AND PLACES OF INTEREST:

Danby Lodge
This magnificent National Park Interpretative and Visitor Centre has a display and exhibitions about the life and landscape of the North York Moors National Park, as well as a programme of events and other publications. There are cafeteria facilities. The centre is open daily in the summer, weekends only in November, February and March (tel: 012876 654).

Egton
One of several attractive villages in Eskdale, it is celebrated for its annual gooseberry fair. Grosmont, just 3km (2 miles) down a steep hill from Egton, is the terminus of the North Yorkshire Moors Railway which runs along the historic Whitby-Pickering railway line through Newtondale to Pickering.

Whitby
This little port on the mouth of the River Esk was long associated with the whaling industry, and many of the fine Georgian and Regency villas on the cliff tops were built for the skippers of successful whaling ships. The story of the town and its epic whaling history is told in the Whitby Museum. The port is also associated with Captain James Cook, discoverer of Australia, who was born close by. In later years, Whitby, with its fine beaches, developed into a popular seaside resort, notable for its Victorian jet jewellery and tasty kippers. No visit to Whitby is complete without climbing the 199 steps past a unique mariners' church, to the spectacular Whitby Abbey, a medieval ruin and the setting for Bram Stoker's grisly tale of the vampire Dracula.

Below: Lealholm Moor, Eskdale. *Author*

Starting Point: Castleton railway station. Four services from Middlesbrough and Whitby (connections at Middlesbrough for Leeds, York and Northallerton). Note: there is no winter Sunday service on the Esk Valley line — ie between the end of September and the end of May.

Finish/Return Point: Whitby railway station: four services a day from Middlesbrough.

Distance: 28km (17 miles).

Map: OS Landranger 94 Whitby.

Surfaces and Gradients: A hilly route, with the longest climb near the start; thereafter short climbs interspersed with long level sections. The surface is tarmac lanes; one short section with a steep descent on a stony track.

Traffic Conditions: Light traffic on quiet lanes — some care is needed in Whitby.

Facilities: Cafés: Danby, Rusarp and Whitby. Pubs: Castleton, Danby, Egton, Ruswarp and Whitby.
Shops: Castleton, Danby and Whitby.
WCs: Danby National Park Centre, Aislaby and Whitby.

Youth Hostel: Whitby (on East Cliff by Whitby Abbey), tel: 01947 602878.

ROUTE INSTRUCTIONS:
From Castleton station entrance turn right into Castleton village, then left towards Danby, keeping directly ahead at the T-junction to Danby village. Cross the lane by Danby station, beside the village green, keeping ahead into the narrow lane opposite. Go over the small hill and on the descent take the left turn signed Danby Beacon (continue a short distance further to go to the National Park Centre). The road climbs steeply up to the moor edge; ignore the turn-offs and continue until the road ends at a T-junction.

Turn left (signed 'Whitby 9'), continuing along the moor before the road dips steeply into a gully and climbs out, then take the first right. This narrow lane follows Eskdale. When you reach a T-junction above Glaisdale turn left, crossing the plateau as far as the next crossroads. Turn right and follow this lane into Egton, then turn right at the junction. Go past the two pubs then take the next left, signed

Below: Whitby harbour. *Author*

Grosmont, and go left again soon after leaving Egton.

Follow this narrow lane, turning right at the next junction to continue along the valley side for the next 4km (2½ miles) to Aislaby.

Joining the wider road in Aislaby, turn right by the toilets on to the bridlepath which descends steeply into Eskdale. Take care, this route is stony and you will probably need to dismount!

Follow the track down to where a tarmac surface begins by some houses and continue descending. At the crossroads go straight ahead for Ruswarp.

In Ruswarp turn right to go over the level crossing then take the first left as the road follows the river and starts ascending. Ignore the turn-off as a short steep climb begins in a side valley.

The road levels out with glimpses of Whitby Harbour before descending. Cross straight over the A171 to continue into the East Harbour. Follow the road round to the west side of the harbour for the station, which is behind the roundabout.

Below: Whitby Abbey. *Peter Waller*

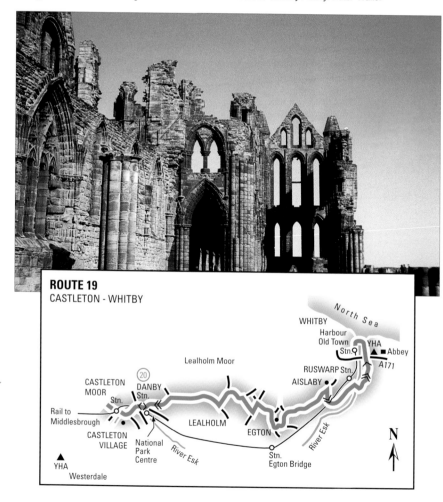

ROUTE 19
CASTLETON - WHITBY

This is a high-level route, taking in some of the best views on offer in the North York Moors. The climb is steady but provides a relatively easy means of crossing the highest part of the moors. By contrast, the first section of the route crosses the flat Vale of Pickering. As the route passes the villages of Normanby and Marton, the plain is interspersed by more and more outlying hillocks of the North York Moors, and you begin to gain height. After crossing the A170 there is a steady climb through Hutton-le-Hole and up Spaunton Moor to the Rosedale Tramway. The route follows this spectacular old mineral railway as far as Blakey Ridge before continuing up to Rosedale Head. With wide views all over the moors and the North Sea coast, the route takes a spectacular descent through the Fryup Valleys and into the Esk Valley.

BACKGROUND AND PLACES OF INTEREST:

Malton (see Route 12)

Hutton-le-Hole
One of the loveliest villages in the North York Moors, with its red pantiled cottages and extended village green, Hutton-le-Hole inevitably attracts tourists and their cars, and therefore has a choice of tea shops, souvenir shops and pubs. It is also the home of the Ryedale Folk Museum, Yorkshire's leading open air museum, with 13 historic buildings illustrating the lives of rural Yorkshire people from prehistoric times to the present day. Open daily during the summer months, tel: 01751 417367.

The Rosedale Railway
Rich deposits of iron ore had been worked in Rosedale since the Middle Ages. As the Teesside iron works boomed in the mid 19th century, the Rosedale branch was opened in 1861 to bring huge deposits of ore out of the mines. This high-level railway was linked to the rest of the railway system by a remarkable incline at Ingleby. At Rosedale Bank Top a steep tramway hauled the iron ore from Rosedale to a furnace where the rock was 'roasted' to burn off excess moisture before transhipment by rail to reduce weight and transport costs. The railway, which closed in 1929, is now a superb level cycling and walking route, with panoramic views into and across Rosedale.

Ralph Crosses
These spectacular crosses were used as preaching places by the early Celtic Christian missionaries, and in later years acted as meeting places, boundary markers and waymarks in otherwise featureless moorland. The Ralph Cross has become the very appropriate emblem of the North York Moors National Park.

Danby
A typical charming Eskdale village with attractive cottages and a small village green. Danby Lodge National Park Centre with facilities is close by (see Route 19).

Below: Rosedale railway track, North York Moors. *Colin Speakman*

Starting Point: Malton railway station. There is an hourly train service from Leeds, with more frequent trains between York and Scarborough; some direct services from Huddersfield and Bradford.

Finish/Return Point: Danby railway station. There are four trains per day to Middlesbrough and Whitby (Esk Valley line). Change at Middlesbrough for an hourly service to Leeds and Huddersfield. NB: There is no winter Sunday service on the Esk Valley line between the end of September and the end of May.

Distance: 50km (30 miles).

Maps: OS 100 Landranger Malton & Pickering, 94 Whitby.

Surfaces and Gradients: One long, steady climb of 260m; otherwise gentle short climbs in the Vale of Pickering and the last part of Rosedale Head. The surface is tarmac lanes and road, with gravel on the Rosedale Railway.

Above: Farndale, North York Moors. *Peter Waller*

Traffic Conditions: First 4km (2³⁄₄ miles) on the B1257 has a steady flow of traffic with some HGVs using the road. The rest of the route is on quiet lanes or on a traffic-free track (the Rosedale Railway).

Facilities: Cafés: Malton, Swinton, Hutton-le-Hole and Danby.
Pubs: Malton, Amotherby, Great Barugh, Normanby, Marton, Hutton-le-Hole, Blakey Ridge (The Lion Inn) and Ainthorpe.
Stores: Malton and Danby.
WCs: Malton (town centre), Hutton-le-Hole (near car park) and Danby Lodge.
YHA: Whitby (tel: 01947 602878).

ROUTE INSTRUCTIONS:
From Malton station entrance turn left and cross the river, then take the right fork, Wells Lane, to the town centre. Turn left then go straight ahead through the traffic lights on to the B1257. Follow this through Broughton and Swinton to Amotherby, turning right. Caution, this road has a

steady flow of traffic, and visibility is restricted at this junction!

The route crosses the flat Vale of Pickering, broken by a short ascent to Great Barugh. Turn left in the village to descend to the River Seven and follow the signs to Kirkbymoorside. At the junction with the A170 (caution when crossing!), go straight ahead to Hutton-le-Hole.

A short drop into the picturesque tourist village of Hutton-le-Hole interrupts the climb; turn right in the upper part of the village on to the Rosedale Abbey road. A steady climb now follows on to the high moors; turn left at the summit on to the track, which is what remains of the Rosedale Tramway.

Follow this track as it runs above Rosedale for 4km (2½ miles), bend left to join the road at Blakey Ridge, below the Lion Inn. Turn right on to the road for the final ascent to Rosedale Head. At the summit turn right (go ahead a short distance if you wish to see the Ralph Cross, the symbol of the National Park) and follow this road around the head of Rosedale. After 2km (1¼ miles) turn left on to the single-track road. This crosses the watershed and there are superb views across the moors and to the coast before the drop into the spectacular Greater Fryup Dale and then into Little Fryup. The lane soon bends round into Eskdale and passes Danby Castle; turn left here to go to Ainthorpe and descend through the village to cross the River Esk. Just over the Esk bridge turn left for Danby station — Danby village lies further ahead.

Below: Farndale, North York Moors, from the Rosedale Tramway. *Author*

ROUTE 20
MALTON - DANBY

Rail to Middlesbrough
DANBY
Stn.
Rail to Whitby
River Esk
To Castleton
Fryup
▲ YHA Westerdale
Rosedale
Rosedale Tramway
Hutton-le-Hole •
KIRKBYMOORSIDE •
A170
NORMANBY •
GREAT BARUGH •
River Rye
Rail to Scarborough
B1257
AMOTHERBY •
A64
Rail to York & Leeds
YHA ▲
Station
MALTON
N ↑

THE HOWARDIAN HILLS: THIRSK TO MALTON

This route combines spectacular views of the White Horse of Kilburn, the ancient Byland Abbey, the grand estates of Newburgh Priory and Castle Howard with the secluded wooded lanes between these sights. After an easy start along the rolling plain of York, the route cuts the edge of the escarpment of the North York Moors to Kilburn and enters the National Park's southwestern corner. Following a secluded valley under the White Horse of Kilburn, the route uses the back lanes through Oldstead to pass the ruins of Byland Abbey. Crossing the gap at Coxwold the route climbs into the relatively unknown Howardian Hills — a low ridge of hills which extends out from the Wolds over the Vales of Pickering and York, with good views of the plains, the southern North York Moors and, in the distance, the Yorkshire Wolds. The lanes climb and dip in the folds of the hills, which change between woodland, open fields and secluded little valleys. After passing the palatial Castle Howard the route rises up again before a long descent into Malton.

BACKGROUND AND PLACES OF INTEREST:

Thirsk
An attractive little market town with several old coaching inns and a large cobbled market place. The veterinary surgery of Alf Wight, better known as James Herriot, is now a museum.

Kilburn
Thomas Taylor, the village schoolmaster of Kilburn, and 30 helpers, carved the white horse out of the hillside in 1857 in imitation of the celebrated White Horse of Uffington, Berkshire. It is a major local landmark, visible from as far away as Harrogate and the Yorkshire Dales. Kilburn was the home of the famous 'Mouseman' wood carver and cabinet maker Robert Thompson. There are several specialist cabinet makers in the Kilburn area.

Coxwold
As well as its fine parish church with an unusual octagonal tower, this pretty village is celebrated as the home of the great 18th-century writer Laurence Sterne, author of the comic masterpiece *Tristram Shandy*.

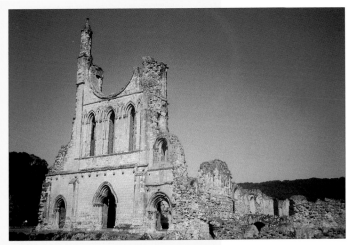

His house, Shandy Hall, which features in
the novel, is now open as a small museum.

Byland Abbey

A group of Cistercian monks, from Furness
Abbey in Cumbria, founded this abbey at
the present site in 1177. It is an impressive
ruin, with the remains of what once was a
magnificent 26ft (8m) rose window. The
ruins are open daily.

Castle Howard

One of England's most spectacular country
homes. Designed by Sir John Vanbrugh with
the help of Nicholas Hawksmoor in 1699 in
grand, baroque style, it took almost half a
century to complete. It is set in beautiful
landscape parkland with a range of obelisks
and other architectural features. Built for
the Earls of Carlisle, it is still the home of
their descendants, the Howard family,
which has given its name to the Howardian
Hills Area of Outstanding Natural Beauty
through which this cycle route passes. The
house and park are open daily to the public
during the summer season.

Malton (see Route 12)

Left: Kilburn White Horse, North York Moors.
Author

Starting Point: Thirsk railway station.
Regular train services from Leeds and York
to Thirsk (Trans-Pennine Express
Middlesbrough or Newcastle trains).

Finish/Return Point: Malton railway station.
An hourly train service from Leeds, with
more frequent trains between York and
Scarborough; some direct from
Huddersfield and Bradford.

Distance: 50½km (31 miles).

Maps: OS Landranger 99 Northallerton &
Ripon, 100 Malton & Pickering.

Surfaces and Gradients: Hilly, with several
short (max 80m) but at times steep climbs;
total climbing 340m. Tarmac lanes
throughout.

Traffic Conditions: There is a short section at
the start on the A61 where traffic is steady;
otherwise quiet lanes throughout.

Facilities: Cafés: Malton and
Byland Abbey.
Pubs: Bagby, Kilburn, Oldstead, Byland
Abbey, Coxwold, Terrington and Malton.
Shops: Thirsk, Kilburn and Malton.
WCs: Thirsk and Malton (town centre).
Youth Hostel: Helmsley (tel: 01439 770433).

ROUTE INSTRUCTIONS:
From Thirsk station turn left on to the A61 into Thirsk. At the roundabout take the second turning signed Sowerby and marked as National Cycle Route NCR 65. Follow this lane through Sowerby to the turn-off left for Bagby. This crosses over the A19, a staggered junction (caution!). Go through Bagby until as far as the T-junction, turning right for Kilburn.

After dipping slightly to cross a stream, the road climbs out of the plain before dropping into Kilburn. Turn left at the edge of the village to follow the lane below the White Horse. Ignore the turn-off and follow the lane to Oldstead; at the Black Swan pub continue straight ahead. This secluded lane emerges at Byland Abbey; turn right to Coxwold. In Coxwold turn left passing the pond of Newburgh Priory before climbing into the Howardian Hills. Soon after reaching the hilltop, turn left and continue to the T-junction. Turn right to Yearsley then left at the crossroads.

Ignoring the turn-off, continue straight ahead then cross straight over the B1363 (taking the right fork at the junction) towards Coulton. The road levels out along a low ridge before descending to the crossroads; turn right to go through the hamlet of Coulton and down the steep gradient (caution!). Note that visibility on this narrow lane is restricted and there is a sharp bend at the bottom. A stiff climb up

the other side of the valley ends in the hamlet of Scackleton; continue to the T-junction. Turn right to go to Terrington, the road dipping and climbing again, before descending through Terrington. 1km (²/₃ mile) after Terrington turn left on to the lane signed for Castle Howard.

Follow this lane to the old gate entrance near Castle Howard and take the Malton road straight ahead. After another climb there is a long gradual descent into Malton. Where the main road is met turn left and continue to the town centre. Just before the traffic lights turn right for the station.

Below: Valley below Coulton. *Author*

ROUTE 21
THIRSK - MALTON

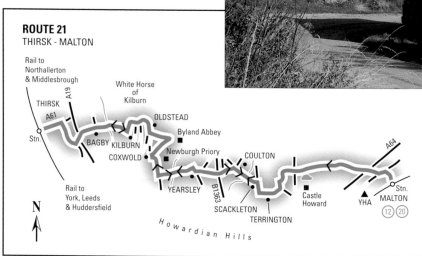

DARTON TO SANDAL VIA ANGLERS COUNTRY PARK, WINTERSETT

This route meanders through gentle, wooded countryside south of Wakefield by the reservoirs and Waterton Country Park Centre at Wintersett. This was once a mining area but already the scars of nearly two centuries of industrial activity have healed and the area is once again returning to its rural beauty and interest. There is a lot to see and do on this short and not-too-strenuous ride, making this an ideal route to tackle with the family.

BACKGROUND AND PLACES OF INTEREST:

Waterton Countryside Discovery Centre
Charles Waterton, an early conservationist, was regarded as eccentric in his day when he built nesting sites for birds and a high wall to keep poachers out. He also constructed a grotto and invited local people to picnic and stroll in the grounds. He provided the inspiration for the Visitor Centre which has an interactive display, activities for children and hides by the lakeside — even binoculars are supplied for the view over the lake should the weather be inclement! The centre is busiest at weekends so if you want a quiet visit try a weekday.

Anglers Country Park
An artificial lake created from open-cast mining in 1982. Today many ducks visit during the winter and it has become one of the most important inland bird sites in West Yorkshire.

Barnsley Canal
Built 200 years ago to carry coal corn and other goods between Wakefield and Barnsley, the canal fell into disuse by the 1950s and has now become a Site of Special Scientific Interest.

Haw Park Wood
Originally part of a much larger woodland, it is now much reduced and replanted with commercial species of larch and pine. However, it is a particularly peaceful and relaxing place to stroll or cycle through.

Below: Road through the woods by Wintersett Reservoir. *Author*

Starting Point: Darton railway station. The MetroTrain Hallam line runs hourly Leeds-Castleford-Wakefield-Barnsley-Sheffield services.

Finish/Return Point: Sandal & Agbrigg railway station: two trains per hour to Wakefield and Leeds; hourly trains to Sheffield and Doncaster.

Distance: 18km (11 miles).

Map: OS 111 Sheffield & Doncaster.

Surfaces and Gradients: One steady climb of 70m, the rest of the route is undulating, mostly downhill. The surface is minor roads

Below: Haw Park Wood, near Waterton Country Park. *Author*

and lanes with one short off-road section on a bridlepath for 2km (1¼ miles) which can be muddy in wet weather. To avoid this, the route can be changed to finish at Fizwilliam station instead.

Traffic Conditions: Back roads and lanes with light traffic — some care is needed in Sandal appraoching the station.

Facilities: Cafés: Mill Lane and Darton (below northbound platform).
For Waterton Countryside Discovery Centre café, check opening times (tel: 01924 863262).
Pubs: Darton, Rose & Crown (at the junction with the A637); Notton, Oliver Twist.
Shops: Bakery at Darton.
WCs: Waterton Countryside Discovery Centre.

ROUTE INSTRUCTIONS:
From Darton station exit turn left on to the B6131. (Caution, this is a fairly busy road!) Ascend the slope and turn left just past the school, going up Sackup Lane. At the hill top, open countryside begins. Cross over Windhill Lane to Warren Lane as the lane goes down to the A61. Turn on to the A61 (take care!), then turn immediately right into a narrow lane bordered by hedgerows. The lane weaves its way down to Notton village. Turn right at the junction.

Go through Notton village and up a slope to cross the B6132 by the Oliver Twist pub. Following the brown signs for the Country Park, continue straight ahead. Go through Old Royston and at the T-junction turn left. (Caution, a few trucks use this minor road!) Continue for ³/₄km (¹/₂ mile), taking the next right. Follow the lane to Ryhill then turn left (at the brown signs for the Country Park) down the narrow wooded lane which runs past the reservoir. Go over the hillock and turn left to Anglers Country Park.

To end the route at Fitzwilliam from Anglers Country Park, retrace the lane back to the junction. Turn left and take the next right to the next junction. Turn left and follow this lane until it meets the B6273. Turn right to follow the B6273 into Fitzwilliam and to the station.

From Anglers Country Park turn right, away from the entrance, to continue along the lane until you reach a gate and the entrance to Haw Park. The route is signed 'Waterton Trail'. The trail is at first surfaced but after it enters the wood it is apt to be muddy after wet weather. Keep to the track, avoiding turn-offs, as it follows the boundary wall before leaving the wood and crossing a field. The route now joins a track

above the Barnsley Canal, which is set in a deep cutting.

Turn right, and follow this track which soon crosses the canal and winds its way across fields, and becomes surfaced. Follow the lane straight ahead as it enters Overtown and Walton, a smart suburb of Wakefield. Go straight ahead at the next crossing and down School Lane which runs under a twin rail bridge before ending at a T-junction. Turn right, between terraced houses, before taking the next left, just after a bus stop. Go down Walton Lane until it meets the traffic lights. Continue straight ahead as far as Pinfold Lane on the right, then take this lane down to meet the main road again. Cross with care to take Agbrigg Road (almost opposite) to Sandal & Agbrigg station (signposted).

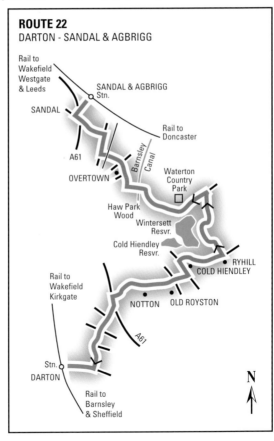

ROUTE 22
DARTON - SANDAL & AGBRIGG

Rail to Wakefield Westgate & Leeds

SANDAL & AGBRIGG Stn.

SANDAL

Rail to Doncaster

A61

Barnsley Canal

OVERTOWN

Waterton Country Park

Haw Park Wood

Wintersett Resvr.

Cold Hiendley Resvr.

RYHILL
COLD HIENDLEY

Rail to Wakefield Kirkgate

NOTTON   OLD ROYSTON

A61

Stn.
DARTON

Rail to Barnsley & Sheffield

N

ROUTE 23

SOUTH YORKSHIRE'S LIMESTONE COUNTRY: KIVETON PARK TO CONISBROUGH (EARTH CENTRE)

A ride through the low hills and valleys of the Magnesian Limestone belt of South Yorkshire. Starting at Kiveton Park, east of Sheffield, this is the southernmost of the routes running close to the Nottinghamshire border. After threading through the villages of Woodsetts and Firbeck the rider passes the ruins of Roche Abbey set in a beautiful little valley. The route gains height towards the hillside village of Hooton Levitt and offers wide views eastward to the Trent Valley and beyond. Dipping down to Maltby, another climb gives fine views west to the Pennine moors, before dropping through the attractive village of Clifton down to Conisbrough in the Lower Don Valley.

BACKGROUND AND PLACES OF INTEREST:

Roche Abbey
Roche Abbey was founded in 1147 by Richard de Bully and Richard FitzTurgis and lies on either side of the stream which divided their land. After the dissolution of the monasteries, the abbey fell into ruins. Capability Brown was responsible for landscaping the grounds in 1774 in its fine setting by limestone cliffs.

The Earth Centre
A fascinating new experience for the millennium, this is an ongoing exhibition complex with a host of practical working examples of sustainable solutions to environmental problems. Part of the exhibition is devoted to enabling the visitor to see and hear the impact our daily lives have on the planet in a unique and provocative gallery which works interactively with the visitor's movements. Other sections have gardens illustrating differing environments (regenerating the barren coal spoil tippings), a tremendously effective water recycling system and an area for children (and adults) which focuses on exploring the senses of hearing and feeling, with unique sculptures. The centre is closed during spring 2000 but much more is to be added for the 2000 season, when it reopens in late summer. For details, tel: 01709 512000.

Conisbrough Castle (see Route 16)

Below: Clifton village, near Conisbrough. *Author*

Right: Conisbrough Castle. *Colin Speakman*

Starting Point: Kiveton Park railway station. Hourly train service from Sheffield to Retford and Lincoln.

Finish/Return Point: Conisbrough railway station. Hourly train service to Sheffield, Doncaster and Hull.

Distance: 32km (20 miles).

Map: OS Landranger 111 Sheffield & Doncaster.

Surfaces and Gradients: Rolling low country for the first half, becoming hillier in the latter stages of the route and ending in a long descent into Conisbrough. The surfaces are tarmac lanes and about 4km (2½ miles) of bridlepaths as well as ordinary roads, so it can get muddy in wet weather at certain points. The potentially worst section, after Maltby, could be avoided by turning off the A631 to Hellaby and rejoining the route at Micklebring.

Traffic Conditions: Mostly quiet lanes and minor roads, but about 3km (1¾ miles) on busier roads.

Facilities: Cafés: Conisbrough, Earth Centre.

Pubs: South Anston, Woodsetts, Firbeck and Conisbrough.
Shops: North Anston, Maltby and Conisbrough.
WCs: Earth Centre.

ROUTE INSTRUCTIONS:
From Kiveton Park station turn right to climb gently out of Kiveton Park. The road soon approaches South Anston; turn right at the T-junction (signed Worksop), then left at the next junction.

Go down the hill to the traffic lights and cross over the A57, and up the other side of the valley. At the crossroads turn right (caution, visibility is restricted here!) and go down the street which narrows to a country lane once the houses are left behind. Further on, the road becomes a bridlepath (a little bumpy on tree roots) which has a narrow section before widening and becoming more grassy as it crosses the fields and descends gently.

By the small wood turn left on to a surfaced path which becomes a back road by the large houses. Turn left up Lindrick Road, which drops down a short slope to a crossroads at Woodsetts. Go straight ahead to pass Gildingwells, and straight ahead again at the crossroads.

At Letwell, after the first sharp bend and just before the next, leave the road to take the dead end road straight ahead — this becomes a track for a short section. Turn left on to the tarmac lane and up the slope to the crossroads. Go straight ahead down the hill to the village of Firbeck. Turn right to head for the A634.

Follow the A634 through the hamlet of Stone to turn off left for Roche Abbey, on a lane — cobbled for part of its way — which drops into a little valley. The entrance to the abbey is on the left as you meet a track. Turn right and continue along the track until it meets the road. Turn left to cross the stream and up the incline to the open fields and Slade Wotton. Turn right here and keep on this road through Hooton Levitt to Maltby.

Turn left on to the A631 (caution, busy road!) and take the third right, by a garage; it is easiest to use the pelican crossing to cross the road. Go up through the estate to the top, then turn left at the T-junction. At the crossroads take the narrow lane straight ahead to follow the ridge top. The lane ends as it drops below a farm; a bridlepath leads to the right of a house which soon widens to a track. This joins a road by a farm; turn right.

Take the next left turn into a lane surrounded by tall hedgerows which leads into Micklebring. At the junction take the Edlington road which crosses the M18 motorway, then turn left for Clifton. Follow the lane down through the village to Conisbrough, going straight ahead at the traffic lights at the foot of the hill. Follow the A6023 round the castle; after 1km (²/₃ mile) Conisbrough station entrance appears on the right. It is probably easier to use the Earth Centre entrance 100m further on where there is both a turning lane and a traffic island — the station is next to the car and cycle park.

Above: Letwell, South Yorkshire. *Author*

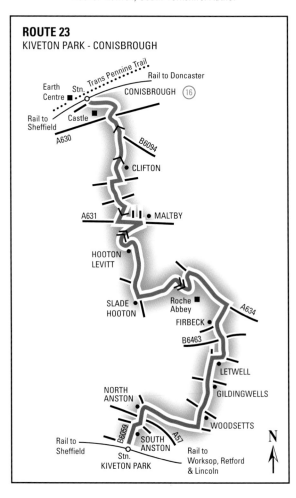

ROUTE 23
KIVETON PARK - CONISBROUGH

THE LOWER AIRE, FAIRBURN INGS AND THWAITE MILLS: GOOLE TO LEEDS

Crossing the southern part of the Vale of York, this route follows the River Aire from its mouth near Airmyn through the flat landscape of mid-Yorkshire with its open fields, small villages and distant power stations. Near Leeds the old industrial landscape has been returned to nature at the bird reserve at Fairburn Ings and a glimpse of the past is possible at Thwaite Mills museum. The canalside part of the route follows the Leeds branch of the Trans-Pennine Trail, blissfully traffic-free until the last short section to the railway station. This route runs east to west — so it can be hard work when cycling into a strong westerly wind. However, navigating through Leeds to the Royal Armouries would be tricky in the other direction.

BACKGROUND AND PLACES OF INTEREST:

Goole
Goole is a large industrial port on the Ouse at its confluence with the Aire & Calder Navigation, the so-called Dutch River. The Aire & Calder, with the Humber, is part of one of Britain's busiest commercial waterway networks. The small museum in Goole Library in the Market Square tells the story of the development of the port.

Carlton Towers
This magnificent mock-medieval Victorian palace, close to the attractive village of Carlton, is the Yorkshire home of the Duke of Norfolk. Its elaborate towers and battlements and its richly decorated rooms were designed by two leading Victorian architects and decorators, Edward Welby Pugin and John Francis Bentley. It is open to visitors in the summer months.

Fairburn Ings
Land subsidence and subsequent floodings created the 'flashes' (ponds) at Fairburn Ings, which is now a regionally important RSPB bird reserve. There are resident and migrant populations of many bird species, including waders, ducks, geese, swans, kingfishers and wagtails — a birdwatcher's paradise. There is a small RSPB information hut close by.

Below: Brewery Wharf, Leeds. *Author*

Thwaite Mills
The unique water-powered 18th century putty mills at this mill complex, with working water wheels and crushing machinery, are rich in industrial and social history. Light refreshments and toilets are available; open daily, except Mondays.

The Royal Armouries and Brewery Wharf
Leeds' newest museum contains major national collections of arms and armour, in stunning displays, linked to a range of changing events. The Brewery Museum close by forms part of the Tetley's brewery complex and illustrates the history of brewing down the ages to the present day.

care is needed as the
road into Castleford,
and to the station, is
busy. There are
frequent trains to
Leeds, and Wakefield
Kirkgate and Barnsley.

Finish/Return Point:
Leeds railway station.
There are hourly local
trains to Doncaster
and hourly services
to Hull.

Starting Point: Goole railway station. There
are regular trains from Doncaster
and Hull but only one train a day direct
from Leeds.

Cut-off Point: Castleford railway station.
Castleford can be reached by turning left at
the traffic lights at Allerton Bywater. Some

Distance: 62km
(38½ miles).

Maps: OS Landranger 105 York & Selby, 104
Leeds & Bradford; OS Leeds Cycling Map.

Surfaces and Gradients: Mostly flat with one
short climb near Fairburn. Be prepared to

Top Left: View of Eggborough power station from Selby Canal. *Author*

Bottom Left: Bridge over the Selby Canal at West Haddlesey. *Author*

Above: Fairburn Ings. *Author*

carry the bike up steps over some bridges along the Trans-Pennine Trail beside the canal. The surfaces are tarmac lanes and roads and a canalside towpath (which is also a footpath).

Traffic Conditions: There is one busy section for 1km (²/₃ mile) along the A614, also a short section crossing the River Aire at Woodlesford on the A624; otherwise the route is on quiet roads and is traffic-free along the Trans-Pennine Trail. Care is needed when crossing busy city centre roads on the last stage of the route.

Facilities: Cafés: Goole and Leeds. Pubs: Goole, Hook, Airmyn, Carlton, Hillam, West Haddlesey, Fairburn, Allerton Bywater and Leeds.

Shops: Goole, Hook, Carlton and Leeds. WCs: Goole, Thwaite Mills and Leeds.

ROUTE INSTRUCTIONS:
From Goole station turn left (under the subway from the Doncaster/Leeds platform) and cross the main road to the pedestrian precinct. Follow the precinct to the roundabout. Take the second turning (by the Yorkshire Bank) and then take the immediate right, Victoria Street. At the end of the street turn and take the bike lane signed for Hook. After a short distance this rejoins the Hook road. Continue into the village of Hook.

At the crossroads turn left on to Church Lane. Follow this as it runs under the M62 motorway bridge, crossing the A614 to Airmyn. Go through the village to reach the A614 again. Turn right (caution, busy road!), and head to the roundabout; take the A645, the second exit (caution, most traffic turns left at this roundabout). (If you wish, you can take the path which is on the right of the road; at the roundabout follow the grass verge round to join the A645 at a safe distance from the junction.)

The A645, although a fast road with HGVs, has more space for cyclists. A few hundred metres after it has crossed over the River Aire take the gated lane (partially hidden) which meets another lane by the houses. Turn right to Carlton.

Cross straight over the A1041 then turn left and then right to emerge at a T-junction. Turn right to thread through the fields, passing a level crossing and some glasshouses. Go straight across the A19 at Chapel Haddlesey and through West Haddlesey to Birkin. Turn right here to head north for 2km (1¼ miles). Turn left at the next junction to go into Hillam. Head for the village centre and at the triangle junction turn left, continuing until the road meets the A162. Turn left on to the A162, but almost immediately turn right (caution, visibility is restricted!) to Fairburn.

After running under a railway bridge the lane ascends gradually to Fairburn. Continue up the slope at the next junction to cross over the A1 then take the next right by the pub. Turn right at the next junction to descend to Fairburn Ings, the wildfowl reserve.

The road runs alongside the ponds and artificial lakes of Fairburn Ings before crossing the A656 at Allerton Bywater. Continue straight ahead, taking the next left fork; this leaves the houses to ascend relandscaped hills. After the road has descended again take the track left, which is the Leeds Country Way. (If there has been a lot of rain this section is muddy and it can be avoided by continuing into Swillington and turning left on to the A642.)

Follow the track round and turn left through the gap on to another track which follows the edge of a wood. Continue until it meets the A642. Turn left to cross the River Aire, and at the next bridge over the Aire & Calder Navigation (canal) look out for the entrance to the Trans-Pennine Trail.

Turn on to the trail, and then turn right to go under the bridge. Follow the trail along the canal; note that at two of the bridges you need to carry your bike up the steps to cross to the other side of the canal. You soon pass Thwaite Mills — to visit the mill complex on its island turn right along the main drive over the canal.

Return to the trail along the towpath between river and canal, pass Knostrop Locks crossing the now combined navigation at Accommodation Road Bridge, then go past the redeveloped areas by the Royal Armouries Museum and Brewery Wharf. From the Royal Armouries go along Clarence Road to the toucan crossing, then down Bowman Lane, turn right to Kendell Street, then left on to Dock Street. Walk across Meadow Lane (care needed!) into Water Street. Take the waterside path in front of the riverside offices to Victoria Road (Caution, cross with care!). Turn right to go under the station along Neville Street to emerge into City Square by the Queen's Hotel station entrance.

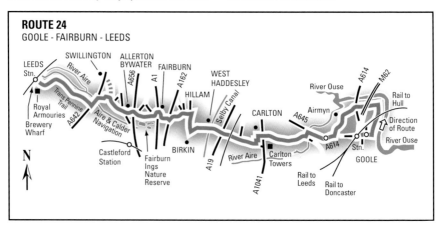

ROUTE 24
GOOLE - FAIRBURN - LEEDS

THE DON GORGE AND CUSWORTH COUNTRY PARK TRAIL: CONISBROUGH (EARTH CENTRE) TO SOUTH ELMSALL

This route passes by some of the best-kept secrets of Doncaster's countryside. It starts on the Trans-Pennine Trail down the wooded Don Gorge, alongside the River Don and Sprotborough Flash Nature Reserve. On reaching the fringes of Doncaster the route then ascends gently through Cusworth Country Park and into the rolling country above the Dearne Valley, passing through woodland and fields with spectacular views across to the Pennines westwards and the flat lowlands to the east. Running through the picturesque old stone village of Hooton Pagnell, a descent is made to South Elmsall on the main railway line between Leeds and Doncaster.

BACKGROUND AND PLACES OF INTEREST:

Conisbrough
Site of a Saxon settlement at nearby Mexborough, a ferocious battle with the Britons in the fifth century resulted in a victory for the Britons and the taking of the fort at Conisbrough. The only Saxon building still standing today is St Peter's Church, built in the 8th century. The imposing Norman castle was built in stone in 1170 by Hamelin Plantagenet.

Cusworth
Just before the entrance to Cusworth Hall is a small church belonging to the Orthodox Coptic community, which is part of the Patriarchate of Alexandria. The Coptic church is a branch of the British Orthodox church. The only thing to distinguish this small Yorkshire stone church is its double cross. Cusworth Hall was

built by George Platt, a local builder and architect, in 1704-45. Managed and run by the local authority since 1961, it is now home to the museum of South Yorkshire Life and is open to the public (Mon-Fri 10am-5pm; Sat 11am-5pm; Sun 1pm-5pm).

Hooton Pagnell
A settlement from the Norman period, it has a hillside location with wide views westwards overlooking the Dearne Valley and the Pennines beyond. The church is completely Norman; Hooton Pagnell Hall has a 14th century gatehouse.

Below: Sprotborough Flash, Don Valley. *Author*

Left: Cusworth Hall. *Author*

Below: Coptic Church, Cusworth. *Author*

Starting Point: Conisbrough railway station and the Earth Centre. Regular trains from Sheffield to Doncaster and Hull call at Conisbrough.

Cut off/Joining Points: The Trans-Pennine Trail can be joined at Doncaster from York Road cycle route or from Bentley. As a variation you can continue on the Cusworth Country Park Cycle Trail as a circular route back to the Trans-Pennine Trial in Doncaster (details on the Cusworth Country Park Cycle Trail from Doncaster Metropolitan Borough Council — see Useful Addresses section).

Finishing/Return Point: South Elmsall railway station. There are hourly trains to Doncaster, Wakefield Westgate and Leeds. Moorthorpe station is further down the road from South Elmsall and has services to Rotherham and Sheffield, also to Leeds if there is a long wait for trains at South Elmsall.

Distance: 26½km (16½ miles).

Map: OS Landranger 111 Sheffield & Doncaster.

Surfaces and Gradients: Easy low rolling country — the first section is flat along the Trans-Pennine Trail — but there are steps (due to be replaced) when leaving the riverside section of the trail. About a third of the route is off-road, and the section between Melton Wood and Hickleton may be muddy. The Cusworth Country Trail, a good part of which is used by this route, is more suitable for mountain bikes.

Traffic Conditions: Much of this route is off-road and the final section is along quiet back roads.

Facilities: Cafés: Earth Centre, Conisbrough and Cusworth Hall.
Pubs: Conisbrough and South Elmsall.
Shops: Conisbrough and South Elmsall.
WCs: Cusworth Hall.

ROUTE INSTRUCTIONS:
From Conisbrough station take the ramp (from the Doncaster-bound platform) down to the river bridge and the Earth Centre. Take the path which leads up the slope by the entrance on to the Trans-Pennine Trail

(TPT). Keep going straight ahead as the path rises a little before descending to the riverside in the Don Gorge.

The TPT follows the river for a few kilometres, passing Sprotborough Flash Nature Reserve before Sprotborough Lock. Continue along the towpath under the high motorway bridge of the A1 and then at the next bridge (of an old railway) take the steps to climb up the embankment, to the old railway trackbed.

Head away from the river as the route passes through the suburban fringes of Doncaster and after open grassland appears on the left turn left at the junction of paths (the junction has the blue bike signs of the Cusworth Country Trail which may be bent in a misleading direction). Follow the path along the hedge then turn left past the waterside cottages, where the track widens and ascends a slope. Turn left on to the road to pass the Coptic church and go up to the entrance of Cusworth Hall. Go through the entrance and follow the track as it ascends into the grounds and the central area of Cusworth Hall.

Leave Cusworth Hall by the drive and the main gate and turn left on to the road. Follow the road under the A1 and shortly afterwards take the right turn, Little Lane, on the bend. Take this road as far as Melton Wood and turn right on to a track which runs along the edge of the wood. The track then turns into the wood through a barrier; continue as far as the junction of several tracks. Take the track left at the 10 o'clock direction, which is a bridleway leading out into an open field.

Cross the field, which can be difficult going as the surface is earthy. At the stone wall turn right and follow the path until it meets a track. Continue in the same direction as the track rises up between open fields and joins a road. Turn left then immediately right to take a wooded track which

runs along a ridge. Bend right where the path splits to maintain height, running through a small wood before joining a minor road. Turn right on to the road and follow it across Hickleton crossroads over the A635 (caution, speeding traffic on the main road!).

Take the next left (signed Cusworth Trail) to Hooton Pagnell, and continue through the village, ignoring right and left turn-offs. Care is needed when the road narrows as it runs through the centre of the village; continue straight ahead (leaving the Cusworth Country Trail which turns off right) to descend the hill to South Elmsall. South Elmsall station is near the centre of the village on the right before the main road junction. Continue straight ahead for Moorthorpe station.

ROUTE 25
CONISBROUGH - SOUTH ELMSALL

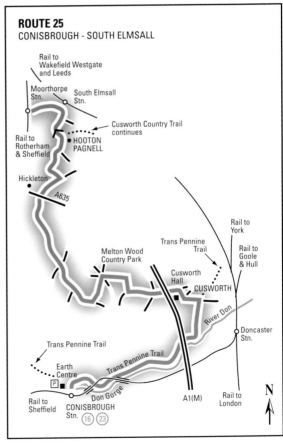

ROUTE 26

YORK TO SELBY

This route uses the Sustrans route along the old York to Selby railway which is now part of the York branch of the Trans-Pennine Trail. Largely traffic-free, the route follows the River Ouse southwards along the low-lying plain of the Vale of York — a landscape of arable fields, small woodlands and open skies. The route begins with the attractive riverside path through York, flavoured with — if the wind is in the right direction — the aroma of the nearby chocolate factory.

BACKGROUND AND PLACES OF INTEREST:

York (see Route 1)

The York-Selby Railway
Formerly the East Coast main line from London to Edinburgh, this was replaced in 1983 when the main line was diverted away from Selby and the new coal mines. The railbed was converted into a cycle track by Sustrans and along the route there are notable sculptures made from machinery reflecting the area's links with mining. A maze is located in a cutting just south of the lane to Escrick.

Selby
This medieval port on the River Ouse has a magnificent abbey church founded in 1069 by the monk Benedict of Auxerre. The railways came early to Selby, a line from Leeds opening in 1834. This was a result of the decision to use the river port to transfer textiles from Leeds on their way to export from Hull. Nowadays Selby is a thriving market town fed by the industries of agricultural processing and the nearby 'superpit' of the Selby coalfield.

Below: Selby-York cycle trail information board. *Author*

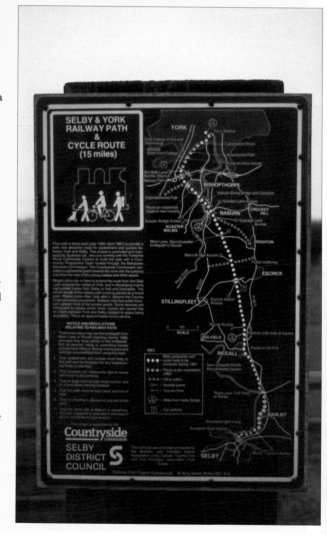

Starting Point: Selby railway station. There are frequent trains to Leeds, Bradford and Halifax; hourly trains to York and Hull.

Finish/Return Point: York railway station. There are frequent trains to Leeds, Huddersfield, Bradford and Halifax; hourly to Hull and Selby.

Distance: 24km (15 miles).

Maps: OS Landranger 105 York & Selby; York & Selby Railway Path & Cycle Route leaflet and map produced by Selby District Council; York City Council cycle map of York.

Surfaces and Gradients: The gradient is flat with a smooth gravel surface along the cycle path; elsewhere there is tarmac along the old A19 (now a back road) and back streets.

Traffic Conditions: Most of this route is off-road; there are short back road sections in Selby, Barlby, Riccall and York.

Facilities: Cafés: Selby and York. Pubs: Selby, Riccall and York. Shops: Selby, Riccall and York. WCs: York.

ROUTE INSTRUCTIONS: From York station it is easier to walk the first hundred metres or so. Cross the road at the station entrance and turn left to follow the path below the city wall, then go under the wall to pass the railway offices, to Tanners Mount, by the pub and cycle park.

Below: Maze on the Selby-York path.
Colin Speakman

From here follow the street round as it bends right to follow the Ouse. After crossing Micklegate at the traffic lights continue straight ahead as the back street soon joins the river, becoming a traffic-free cycle and pedestrian path.

The riverside cycle path bends left up an embankment and joins a small back road; continue left, going along the side of the racecourse. At the next junction turn sharp left to go under the bridge. The path follows the side of the A64 York bypass before descending to another junction. Turn left under the road tunnel to join the old railway trackbed.

The route passes through a housing estate in Bishopthorpe, turning right to follow an estate road for a short distance before rejoining the old trackbed. The route now follows the route of the East Coast main line, taking a very straight course.

Passing the maze near the Escrick road, the path uses the old trackbed as far as Riccall, where the A19 occupies the line, so the route turns and runs through the village. The route then runs alongside the A19 as a

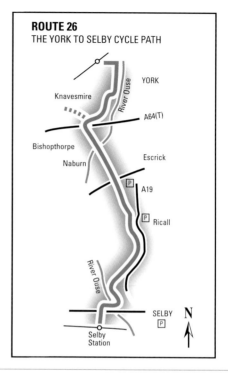

ROUTE 26
THE YORK TO SELBY CYCLE PATH

St Mary's Abbey, York. *Colin Speakman*

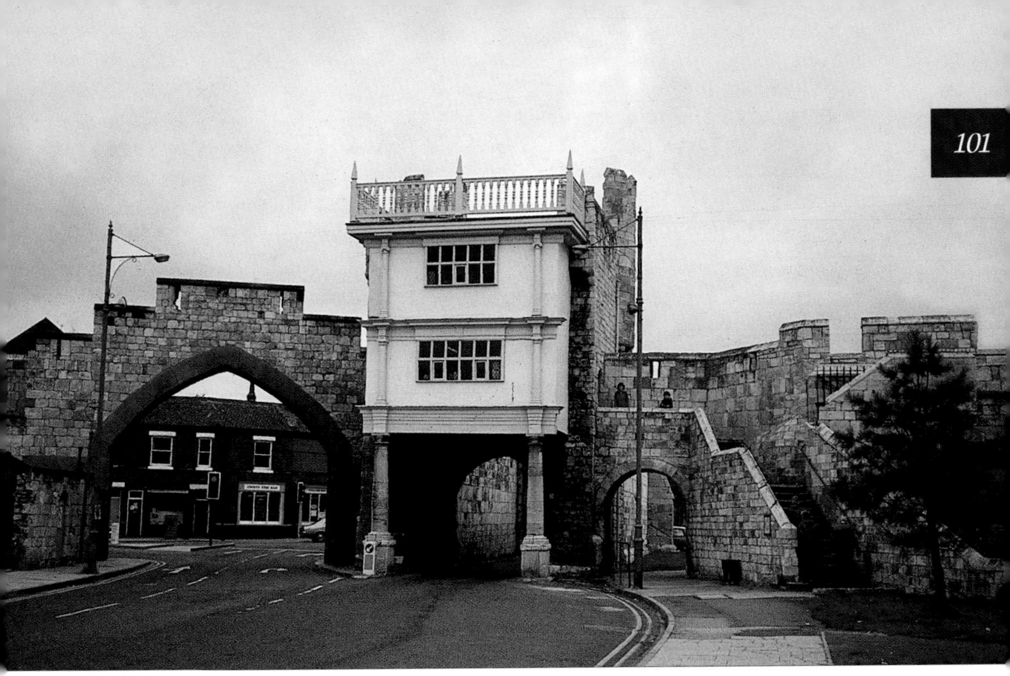

cycle path. After about 1km (¾ mile), the bike route turns right again to go on a back road through Barlby. Follow this until the roundabout where the path turns to the right, marked by blue bike path signs.

The route into Selby town centre goes along the river bank and runs by the Rank Hovis river frontage, before dropping down the embankment. Follow Bungalow Road, taking Pond Street (fourth left) then turn right on to the main road to cross by the old toll bridge. Take the next left to reach the station.

Above: Bootham Bar, York. *Colin Speakman*

Below: Holy Trinity Church, Godram Gate, York. *Peter Waller*

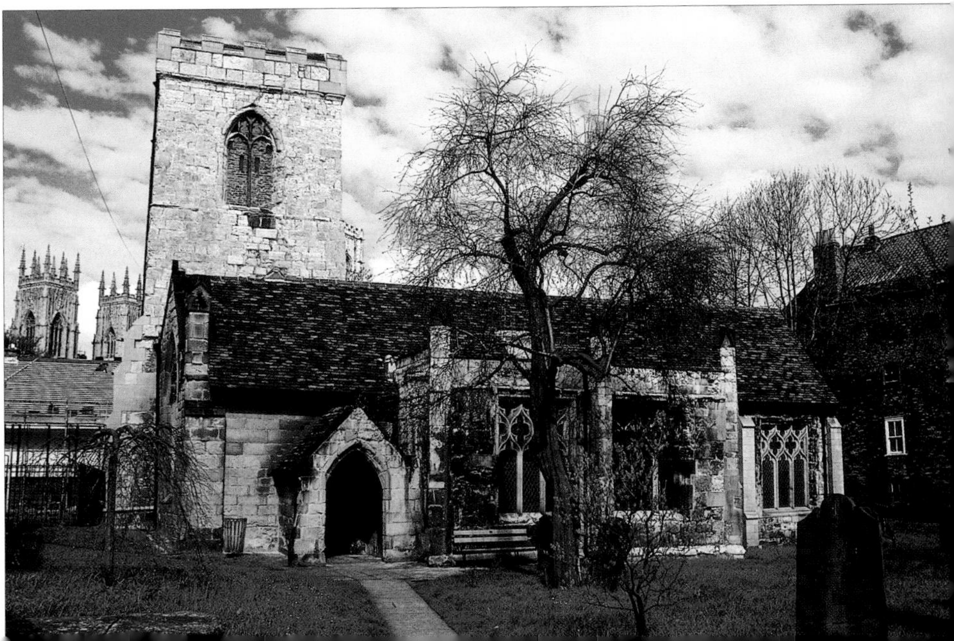

THE SCARBOROUGH TO WHITBY TRAILWAY

The Scarborough-Whitby Trailway in the North York Moors National Park follows the line of the old Scarborough to Whitby railway along a spectacular route around the North Sea coast, known as the North Yorkshire Heritage Coast. It offers some dramatic views over such famous landmarks as Robin Hood's Bay, Boggle Hole and Whitby Abbey. This cycle route is probably one of the most scenic in the North of England, serving an area mostly inaccessible by road, across undulating pasture and wooded dales, skirting the edge of some of Britain's grandest cliffs.

BACKGROUND AND PLACES OF INTEREST:

The Scarborough-Whitby line was opened in 1885, having taken 13 years to build, and represents a dramatic piece of engineering which includes the 13-arched, 915ft-long viaduct over the River Esk and the climb between Robin Hood's Bay and Ravenscar, once one of the steepest gradients on English railways at 1 in 39. Not only did the line cost substantially more than was envisaged, with many investors losing money, but it was never profitable and finally closed in 1965.

Scarborough
An elegant seaside resort with fine beaches and attractive promenades, Scarborough was a fashionable Victorian watering place popular for its sea-bathing and fresh air. Today, Scarborough is still a popular seaside destination, with visitors also enjoying its pleasant parks and clifftop walks. The town is dominated by its 12th century castle, now in the care of English Heritage. The castle is open 10am-6pm from 1 April to 31 October, and 10am-4pm from 1 November to 31 March (Wed-Sun). There is an admission charge.

Ravenscar
From Ravenscar there are some dramatic views over Robin Hood's Bay. The National Trust own over 10 miles of the North Yorkshire and Cleveland Heritage Coast, including this section. An introduction to

Below Left:
Scarborough-Whitby
Trailway.
Lydia Speakman

Right: The Heritage
Coast from the
Scarborough-Whitby
Trailway.
Lydia Speakman

the coast is provided in a series of exhibitions at the Coastal Centre (open daily from Easter to the end of September) which stands adjacent to the trailway. At Ravenscar the railway went through a 279yd-long tunnel which was built on the wishes of one of the directors of the line who owned Raven Hall and didn't wish the line to obscure his view of the coast. In the 1890s there were plans to develop Ravenscar as a seaside resort. Roads, a water supply and drains were laid and over 1,500 plots offered for sale, but in this rather windswept location the idea never caught on.

Peak Alum Works
Close to the trailway, linked by a footpath, lies the Peak alum works which were founded in 1650 and eventually closed in 1862. Alum was used for fixing cloth dye and tanning leather. Ships moored at a purpose-built jetty to bring in iron, lead and barrels of urine — an essential ingredient in the alum-making process. The alum works have now been restored by the National Trust.

Robin Hood's Bay
Known locally as Bay or Bay Town, Robin Hood's Bay is a delightful collection of tightly packed houses and narrow streets connected by narrow, cobbled passageways and short flights of steps. Standing huddled against the sea, the brightly coloured cottages, with their pantile roofs and tiny wooden porches, were said to have been built close together so that the women would have company when the men were away at sea. Once a thriving fishing centre, in the 17th and 18th century Robin Hood's Bay was also a haven for smugglers. It is said that a bolt of silk could be passed from the houses near the sea to the cliff top via interconnecting doors and cellars without it seeing daylight.

Whitby
An attractive fishing town, based around a harbour from which lead narrow cobbled streets. Whitby is famous for its jet, a black stone found only in and around the town, which became popular in Victorian times when it was elaborately carved into cameos and other pieces of jewellery. Standing above the town and reached by 199 steps, is Whitby Abbey, an ancient holy place and once the burial place of kings. The abbey was host to the famous Synod of Whitby in the 7th century, presided over by Abbess Hilda, where the Roman and Celtic churches agreed the date of Easter. The remains of the abbey are mainly the Benedictine church of the 13th and 14th centuries. It is open daily 10am-6pm (10am-4pm October-March) with an admission charge.

Starting Point: Scarborough railway station. There are regular trains from Leeds; less frequent direct services also run from Huddersfield, Halifax and Bradford.

Finish/Return Point: Whitby. There are four trains per day to Middlesbrough from Whitby (Esk Valley line). Change at

Above: Whitby Abbey and harbour. *Author*

Middlesbrough for an hourly service to Leeds and Huddersfield. NB: There is no winter Sunday service on the Esk Valley line — ie between the end of September and the end of May.

ROUTE 27
THE SCARBOROUGH - WHITBY TRAILWAY

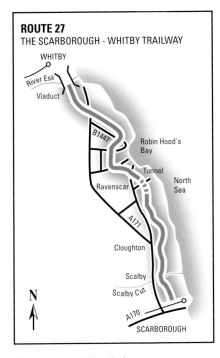

Distance: 29km (18 miles).

Maps: OS Landranger 101 Scarborough, 94 Whitby.

Surfaces and Gradients: The gradients on the old railway trackbed are easy. Surface conditions vary from rough path to smooth gravel. The route is currently suitable only for mountain bikes, although Scarborough District Council intends to improve the track in the coming years.

Traffic conditions: Much of this route is off-road and the final section is along quiet back roads.

Facilities: Cafés: Scarborough, Ravenscar, Robin Hood's Bay and Whitby.
Pubs: Scarborough, Ravenscar and Robin Hood's Bay.
Shops: Scarborough and Whitby.
WCs: Scarborough and Whitby.

From Scarborough railway station turn left on to Westborough Road and right on to West Parade. The trail starts at the far end of the Safeway's car park where a tarmac path follows the line of a former cutting through northern Scarborough, passing a cemetery and continuing along the edge of a housing estate, towards Scalby.

The trail continues to Scalby where the route crosses the Scalby Cut on a brick viaduct. From the viaduct continue up Chichester Close to the road. Cross the road and then turn up Field Close Road on the opposite side of the road and then right along Lanchester Way to rejoin the trail.

The trail carries on to the outskirts of Cloughton where it deviates from the former trackbed through the old goods yard, and then continues to Staintondale and Ravenscar.

At Ravenscar the original tunnel has been closed and the trail continues along a minor road through the village. Where the road swings sharply left, continue down a rutted track which is signposted to rejoin the old railway just north of the tunnel entrance. The trail continues to Robin Hood's Bay, where part of the trackbed is used as a linear car park.

The trail ends at Esk Viaduct 2¼km (1½ miles) from Whitby, where there is a path from the embankment down to the road below. Cyclists wishing to continue to Whitby should turn right along the road to where the road meets the main A171 road at a crossroads. Continue straight ahead following the River Esk to the East Harbour, following the road round to the West Harbour and the railway station in the centre of Whitby. For those cyclists preferring to end their journey at Ruswarp (railway station 1km [¾ mile] distant) turn left along the road to where it meets the B1416 and cross a bridge over the River Esk. Ruswarp station is on the right-hand side.

As well as the National Cycle Routes, there are a growing number of cycle routes being built by various local authorities. Leading lights in Yorkshire are the cities of York and Hull, who also supply maps of their city networks. Others such as Leeds, Doncaster and Sheffield, are beginning to make some effort to develop cycle routes, with varying degrees of success; other authorities such as Wakefield, Scarborough and the East Riding of Yorkshire councils are (or have been) developing some recreational routes, and other areas promote the use of bridlepaths for recreational cycling. Below is a list of what is available from local authorities, British Waterways and the Forestry Commission.

Useful contact numbers are given at the end of this section.

LOCAL AUTHORITY ROUTES

East Yorkshire

Hull-Hornsea Rail Trail: An attractive 19km (11-mile) route following the line of the old railway linking the coastal resort of Hornsea with the centre of Hull.

Hull-Trans-Pennine Trail: see unofficial guide to Trans-Pennine Trial.

Market Weighton-Bubwith: A 19km (12-mile) railway path route from the East Yorkshire Wolds to the Vale of York.

North Yorkshire

Scarborough-Whitby: A 32km (20-mile) route using the old railway line running parallel to the coast joining the two famous resorts. Currently the conditions of the track are described by the council as poor, but it is planned to improve its state.

Selby-Howden: A link route from Selby (Route 3) to Howden in East Yorkshire, not far from Goole (Route 24).

Yorkshire Dales Cycleway: Route running 210km (130 miles) along the back roads of the Yorkshire Dales.

Below: The White Rose Cycle Route. Sustrans/John Murray

Below Right: The Harland Way, near Wetherby. Author

South Yorkshire

Doncaster — Cusworth Country Park Cycle Trail: A circular 23½km (15-mile) route using lanes and bridlepaths around Cusworth Country Park west of Doncaster; links with the Trans-Pennine Trial (within easy distance of Conisbrough's Earth Centre and Routes 16 and 23 in this book).

Doncaster — Hatfield Water Park: A circular trail around Hatfield; details from Doncaster Metropolitan Council Leisure Services.

Rotherham — Round Rotherham Rides: Rotherham Metropolitan Council produces useful waterproof cards with six rides around the district along back roads and bridlepaths. (Route 23 uses a good part of one of the routes.)

Sheffield: Routes are being developed in the Sheffield area at the time of writing. Contact Sustrans or Sheffield City Council for further details.

West Yorkshire

Calderdale — Mountain Bike Trails in Upper Calderdale: Short and long routes mapped out by Calderdale Council. A route along the Calder Valley is planned for 2000.

Kirklees (Huddersfield & Dewsbury districts): A series of leaflets called 'Record Breaking Rides' gives some suggestions for circular rides. Contact Kirklees Countryside Unit, tel: 01484 443704.

Leeds — East End Park-Osmondthorpe-Halton Moor-Temple Newsam-Colton: An off-road route running through the southern part of East Leeds — access to East End Park is tricky from the city centre but the route can be accessed from other parts of East Leeds and Cross Gates (see Route 3).

Leeds — Middleton Park (with link to Wakefield): A South Leeds route from the centre.

Leeds — Town Hall-University-Hyde Park-Headingley: A signed, mostly on-road route using back streets.

Leeds and Bradford: see British Waterways Leeds & Liverpool canal.

Wakefield: A map of recreational routes is available from Wakefield Metropolitan Council.

The West Yorkshire Cycle Route: A 150-mile route around West Yorkshire mainly on

FORESTRY COMMISSION

There are also a number of additional routes through Forestry Commission land. These include:

Boltby Forest: Offers one route.

Cropton Forest: An off-road route from Levisham station on the North Yorkshire Moors Railway exploring the forest.

Dalby Forest: Offers one route.

Guisborough Forest: Offers one route.

For details of these and other areas where cycling is permitted contact: Forest Enterprise, North Yorks Moors Forest District, 42 Eastgate, Pickering, North Yorkshire YO18 7DU, tel: 01751 472771/473810.

Above: Trans-Pennine Trail, near Wombwell. *Author*

Top Right: River Wharfe and Wharfedale hills, near Barden. *Author*

Bottom Right: Cyclists on the Harland Way, Wetherby. *Colin Speakman*

quiet lanes and bridleways with some short sections on bridleways. A leaflet is available from local tourist offices describing the route. Beware — some of the sections are extremely hilly!

CANAL TOWPATHS AND THE REGIONAL BRITISH WATERWAYS BOARD

Cycling is allowed along the following canals within the region:

The Aire & Calder Navigation Canal: Leeds-Woodlesford.

The Leeds-Liverpool Canal: Leeds-Apperley Bridge (permission is required to reach Shipley, Bingley and Skipton — see below).

For further information contact the local British Waterways Board Office: Northeast Regional Office, 1 Dock Street, Leeds 1HH (tel: 0113 243 6741); Leeds-Liverpool (East) Dobson Lock, Apperley Bridge, Bradford BD10 0PY (tel: 01274 611303).

FURTHER INFORMATION  *109*

Calderdale Biking Guide: Pocket Rides (2) by Paul Hannon, published by Hillside Publications (1996). Mostly includes off-road sections.

Cycle Routes in West Yorkshire by Derek Purdy, published by Ernest Press (1998).

Cycling Without Traffic: North by Colin & Lydia Speakman, published by Dial House (1996).

Huddersfield Examiner: Rural Rides: 12 routes in and around Huddersfield by Mel Gibson, available in local bookshops and *Huddersfield Examiner* offices.

Record Breaking Cycle Trails: A series of leaflets available from Kirklees Countryside Unit, tel: 01484 443704.

Round Rotherham Rides: A series of laminated leaflets available from Rotherham

Metropolitan Council,
tel: 01709 822022.

Ryedale Mountain Bike Routes (North Yorkshire):
A set of four routes exploring the countryside around Malton; leaflet available from Ryedabike (tel: 01653 692835) at a small charge.

West Yorkshire Cycleway:
Leaflets available in most Tourist Information Centres.

The White Rose Cycle Route:
Hull to Middlesbrough, published by Sustrans (tel: 0117 929 0888).

Yorkshire Dales Cycleway:
Separate guides available from National Park Information Centres and Sustrans.

Right: Hawes, old courtyard. *Author*

Below: Ilkley Old Bridge, Wharfedale. *Author*

Council Cycling Departments

East Yorkshire:
East Riding County Council;
tel: 01482 884430
Hull City Council, c/o Leisure Services Dept;
tel: 01482 223559

North Yorkshire:
Scarborough Borough Council, c/o Dept of
Technical Services; tel: 01723 232323
Selby District Council, c/o Economic
Development Office; tel: 01757 292005
York Cycle Officer; tel.: 01904 613161

South Yorkshire:
Barnsley Metropolitan Council (as Trans-
Pennine Trail contact); tel: 01226 772574
Doncaster Metropolitan Council, c/o Leisure
Services; tel: 01302 737343
Rotherham Metropolitan Council
Countryside Service; tel: 01709 822022

West Yorkshire:
Bradford Metropolitan Council, c/o Design &
Construction Services; tel: 01274 757648
Calderdale Metropolitan Council, c/o Leisure
services Countryside Access;
tel: 01422 886149
Kirklees Metropolitan Council, c/o Highways
Dept; tel: 01484 225638
Leeds City Council Cycling Dept;
tel: 0113 247 6385
Wakefield Metropolitan Council (Traffic &
Transportation Group); tel: 01942 306066

National Parks Information
North York Moors; tel: 01439 770657; website:
http://www.northyorkmoors-npa.gov.uk
Yorkshire Dales; tel: 01756 752748; website:
http://www.yorkshiredales.org.uk

Travel Information
Countrygoer website (information on access
to the countryside);
ttp://www.countrygoer.org.uk
National Rail Enquiries; tel: 0845 748 49 50
Northern Spirit; tel: 0870 602 3322; website:
http://www.northern-spirit.co.uk/
Railtrack National Rail Enquiries website;
http://195.92.21.203/bin/query.exe/en
South Yorkshire PTE; tel: 01709 515151
West Yorkshire Metro; tel: 0113 245 2676;
website: http://ukbus.u-net.co.uk

Weather Information
Meteorological Office forecast for Yorkshire:
http://www.meto.gov.uk/datafiles/RYPMS.html

Other Useful Organisations

Bike Rail Group; tel: 0973 828163

British Cycling Federation and British
Mountain Bike Federation; The National
Cycling Centre, 1 Stuart Street, Manchester
M11 4DQ; tel: 0161 223 2244

The Cycle Campaign Network, c/o London
Cycling Campaign; 2 Stamford Street,
London SE1 9NT

The Cyclists Touring Club (CTC); Cottrell
House, 69 Meadrow, Godalming, Surrey
GU7 3HS; tel: 01483 417217

Earth Centre; tel: 01709 322 085; website:
http://www.earthcentre.org.uk

Environmental Transport Association (ETA);
The Old Post House, Heath Road, Weybridge,
Surrey KT13 8RS; tel: 01932 828882

Friends of TPT; Trevor Blackburn,
164 High Street, Hook, Goole DN14 5PL

Sustrans National Office; 35 King Street,
Bristol BS1 4DZ; tel: 0117 929 0888; website:
http://www.sustrans.org.uk

Trans-Pennine Trail (TPT); c/o Barnsley MBC,
Central Offices, Kendray Street,
Barnsley S70 2TN; tel: 01226 772574

Transport 2000; The Impact Centre,
12-18 Hoxton Street, London N1 6NG;
tel: 020 7613 0743

Youth Hostels Association National Office;
8 St Stephens Hill, St Albans, Herts AL1 2DY;
tel: 01727 855 215

INDEX

Illustrations listed in italics.